Banjo Picking Tunes

FUN SOLOS TO PLAY

by Lluís Gómez

To access the online audio go to:

WWW.MELBAY.COM/30905MEB

The Prucha Spirit Jason Burleson Signature Model banjo cover image courtesy of Prucha Bluegrass Instruments.

© 2020 By Mel Bay Publications, Inc. All Rights Reserved.

WWW.MELBAY.COM

Contents

Title	Page	Audio
Cumberland Ridge	4	1
Caleb's Gorge	4	2
Far from Home	5	3
The Teetotaller's Reel	6	4
Swallowtail Jig	7	5
Morrison's Jig	8	6
The Cuckoo	9	7
Barney's Goat	9	8
The Clergy's Lamentation	10	9
Red Fox Waltz	11	10
The Downfall of Paris	12	11
Reel de Lapin	13	12
Eleven Mile Canyon	14	13
The Burning of the Piper's Hut	15	14
Young McGoldrick	16	15
Jackson's Jig	17	16
Little House 'Round the Corner	18	17
Missouri Mud	19	18
Whiskey Before Breakfast	20	19
Neapolitan Threshers	21	20
Eighth of January	22	21
Harvest Moon Strathspey	23	22
Buttermilk Jig	24	23
An Comhra Donn	25	24
National Lancer's Hornpipe	26	25
Brighton Beach	27	26
Green Fields of America	28	27
St. Clair's Hornpipe	29	28
Star of Bethlehem	30	29
Bennett's Favorite Reel	31	30
Ivy Leaf Reel	32	31
St. Anne's Reel	33	32
Gladiator Reel	34	33
Luckie Bawdin's Reel	35	34
Witch of the Wave Reel	36	35
North Sea	37	36
Red Haired Boy	38	37
Mere Point	39	38
Blackberry Blossom	40	39
Wilson's Hornpipe	42	40
Carolan's Draught	44	41
Days of 'Lang Syne	45	42
Brush Creek	46	43
The Rights of Man	47	44
The Unfortunate Rake	48	45
Shannon's Well	49	46
Lark in the Morning	50	47
Author Bio	51	
Index of Solos	52	

Preface

This collection of 47 tunes was derived from the rich traditions of American, Irish and Scottish folk music with a few original melodies contributed by William Bay and Turlough O'Carolan. With intermediate-level players in mind, the music is presented in banjo tablature with suggested accompaniment chords.

The selections in this book are intended to be played in the innovative styles of Earl Scruggs, Bill Keith and Don Reno, that is, with picks on the thumb, index and middle fingers. If you are not familiar with the work of these three pioneering banjoists, I suggest you learn more about them; doing so will help you play the tunes in this book and better inform you of the amazing history of our beloved instrument.

The tunes themselves are relatively unadorned and straightforward but contain some intricate fingering to challenge and improve your technique. Together with the chord symbols, however, they can also be used for group jamming or solo improvisation.

While all of the tunes are written in standard G tuning (gDGBD), you'll notice that some of them sound in the keys of E or A without using a capo. For example, "Red Haired Boy" is in the mixolydian mode of A [the dominant or 5th degree of the D major scale] which contains a G-natural rather than a G-sharp.

It is very important that you listen to the audio recordings to learn and master these tunes at a slow to moderate tempo before trying to play them at full speed. Find different ways to approach each melody, and experiment and improvise to create your own arrangements.

Have fun and keep at it!

Lluís Gómez

Recorded by Lluís Gómez at Dotze Contes Studio
Mastering by Jordi "Kako" Vericat at JK Music
Lluís Gómez plays and endorses Prucha Banjos.

Cumberland Ridge

Traditional
Arr. Lluís Gómez

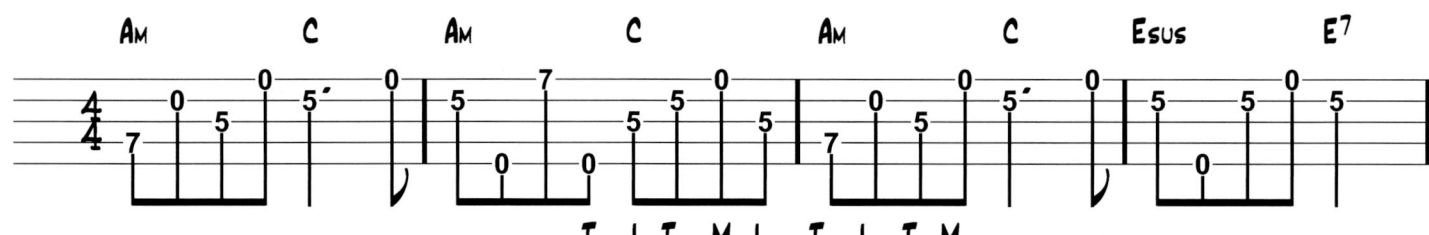

Caleb's Gorge

Traditional
Arr. Lluís Gómez

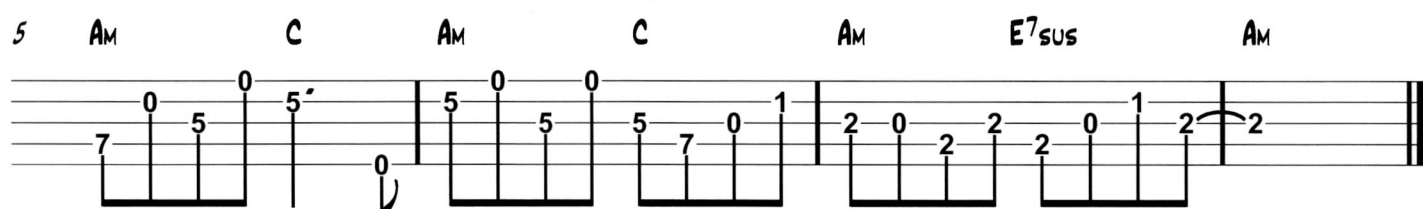

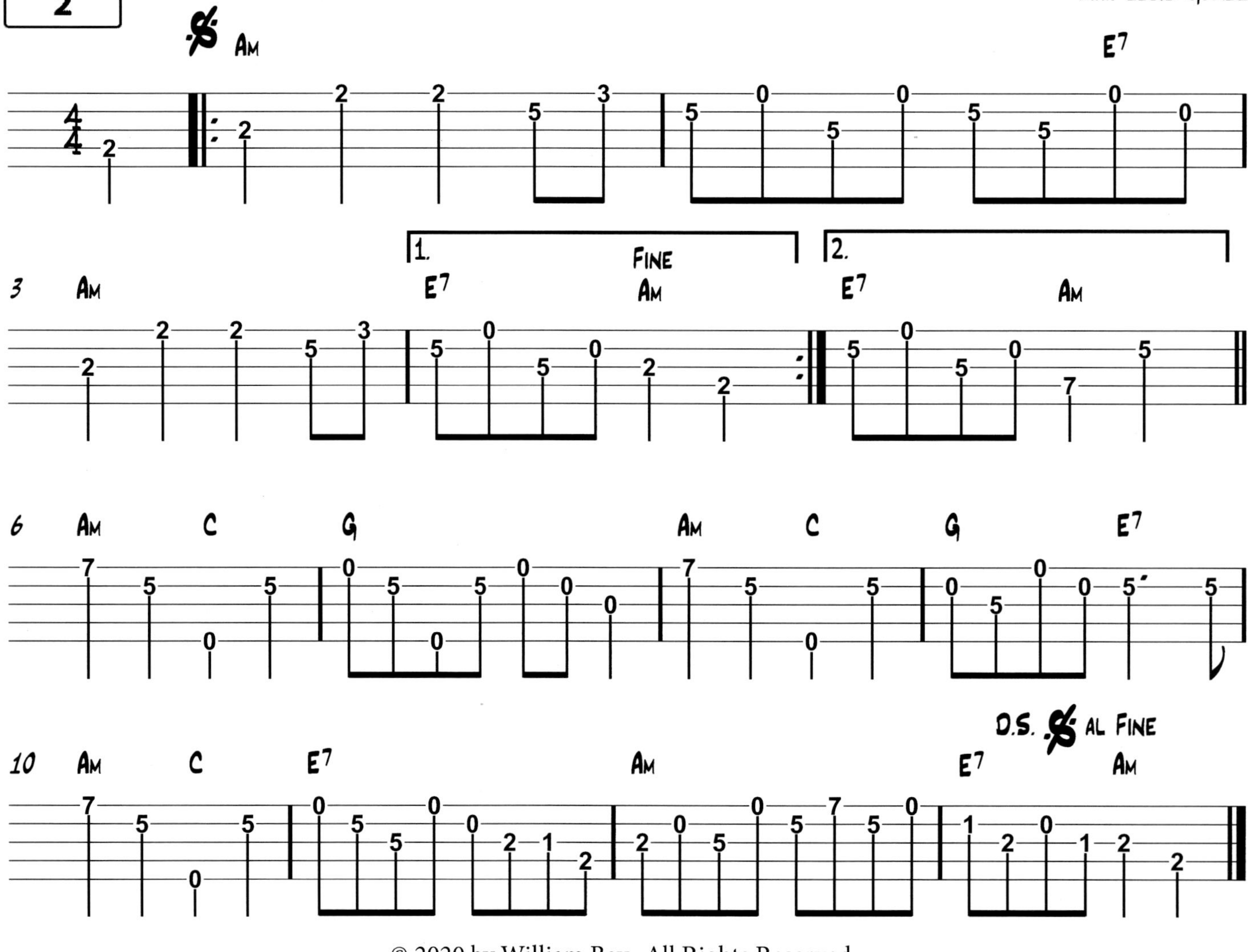

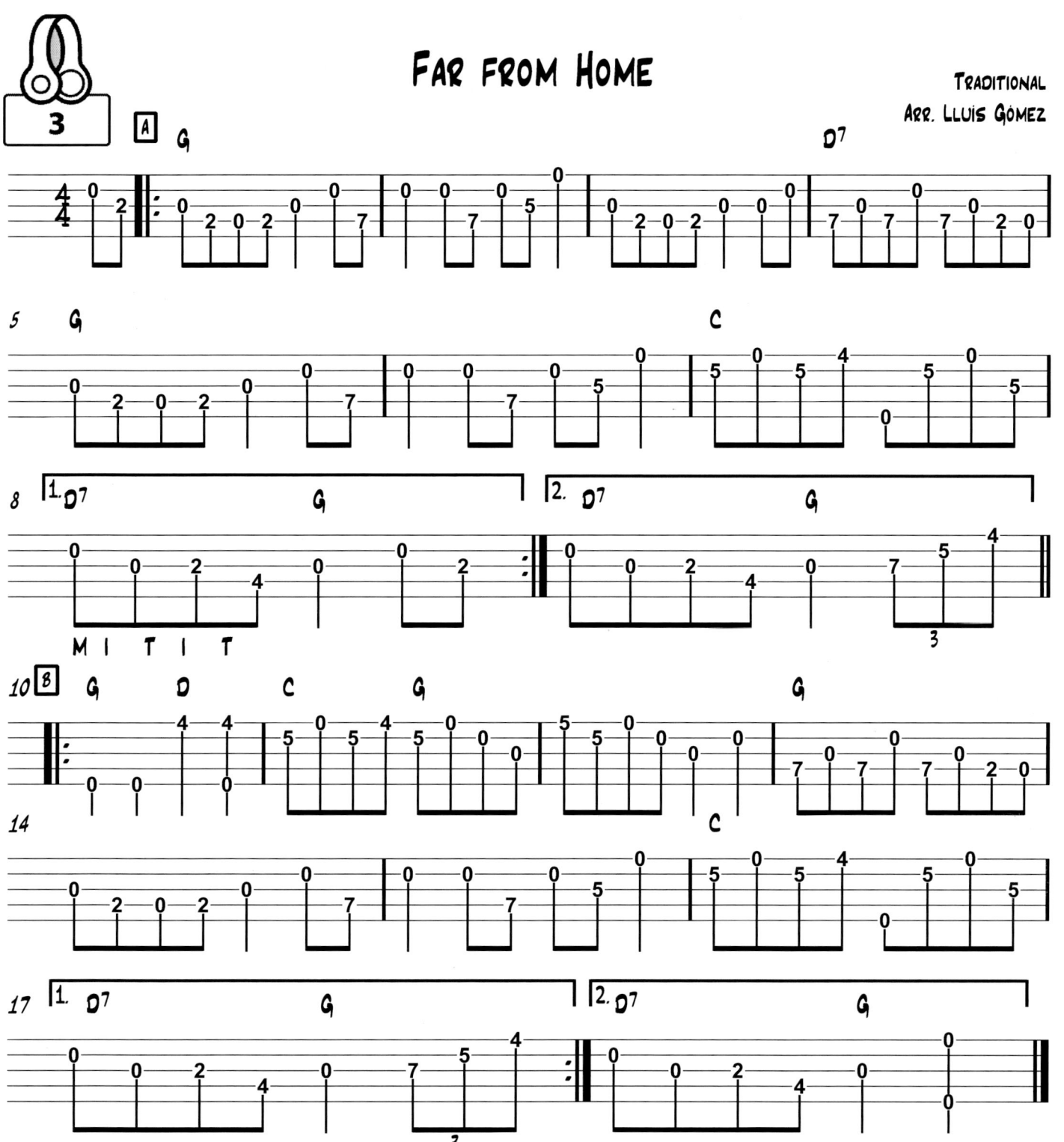

The Teetotaller's Reel

Traditional
Arr. Lluis Gómez

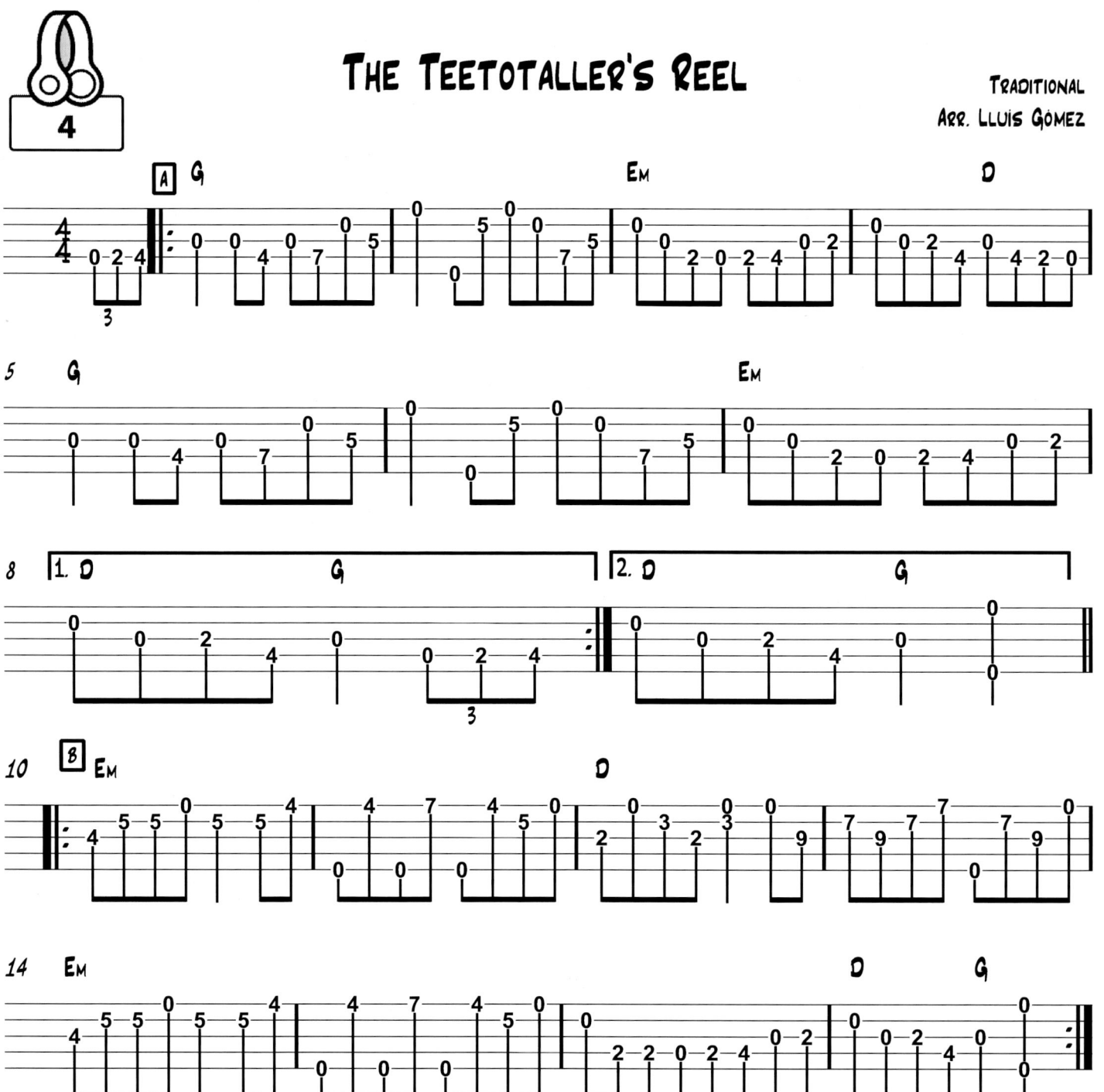

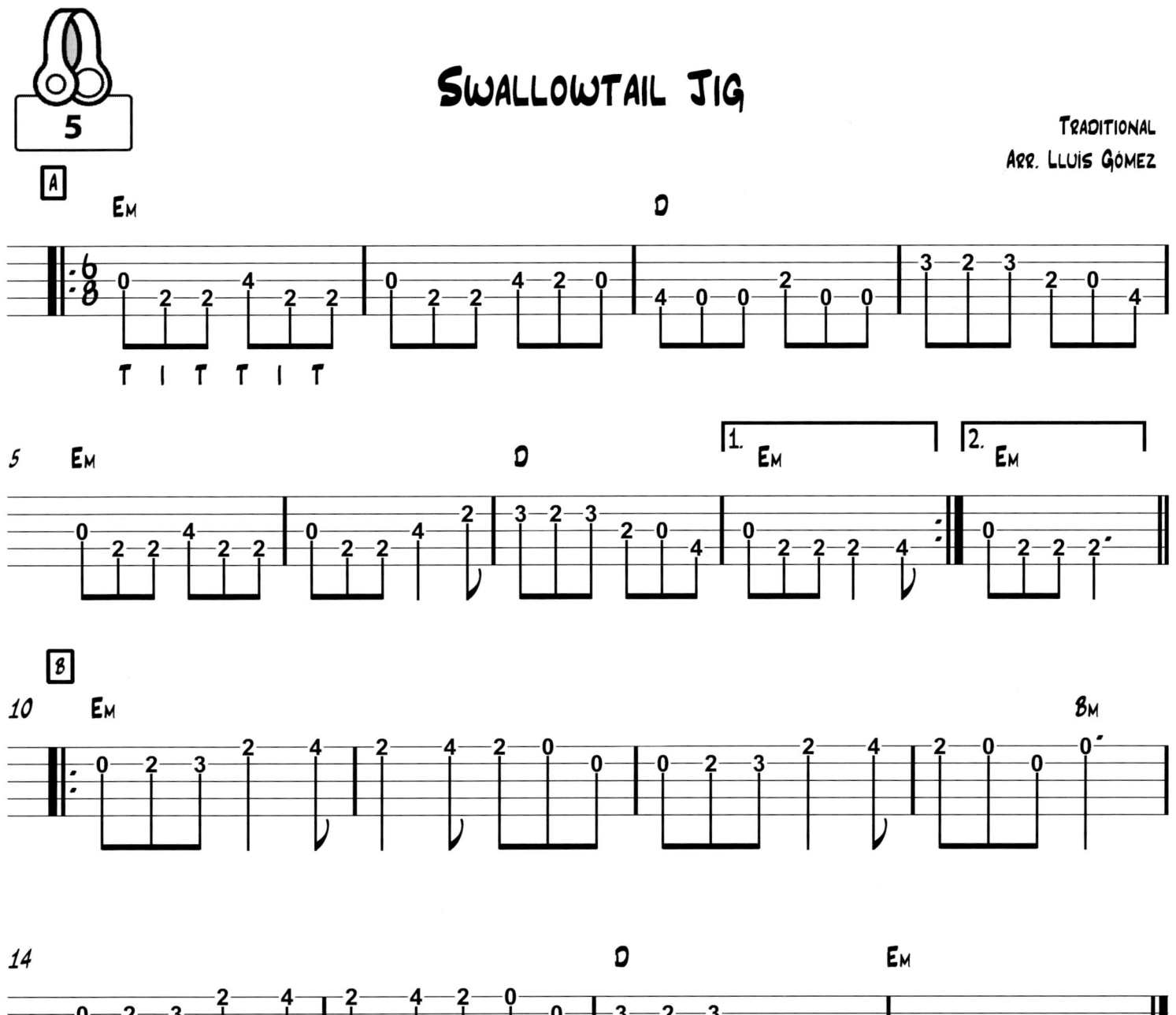

Morrison's Jig

Traditional
Arr. Lluis Gómez

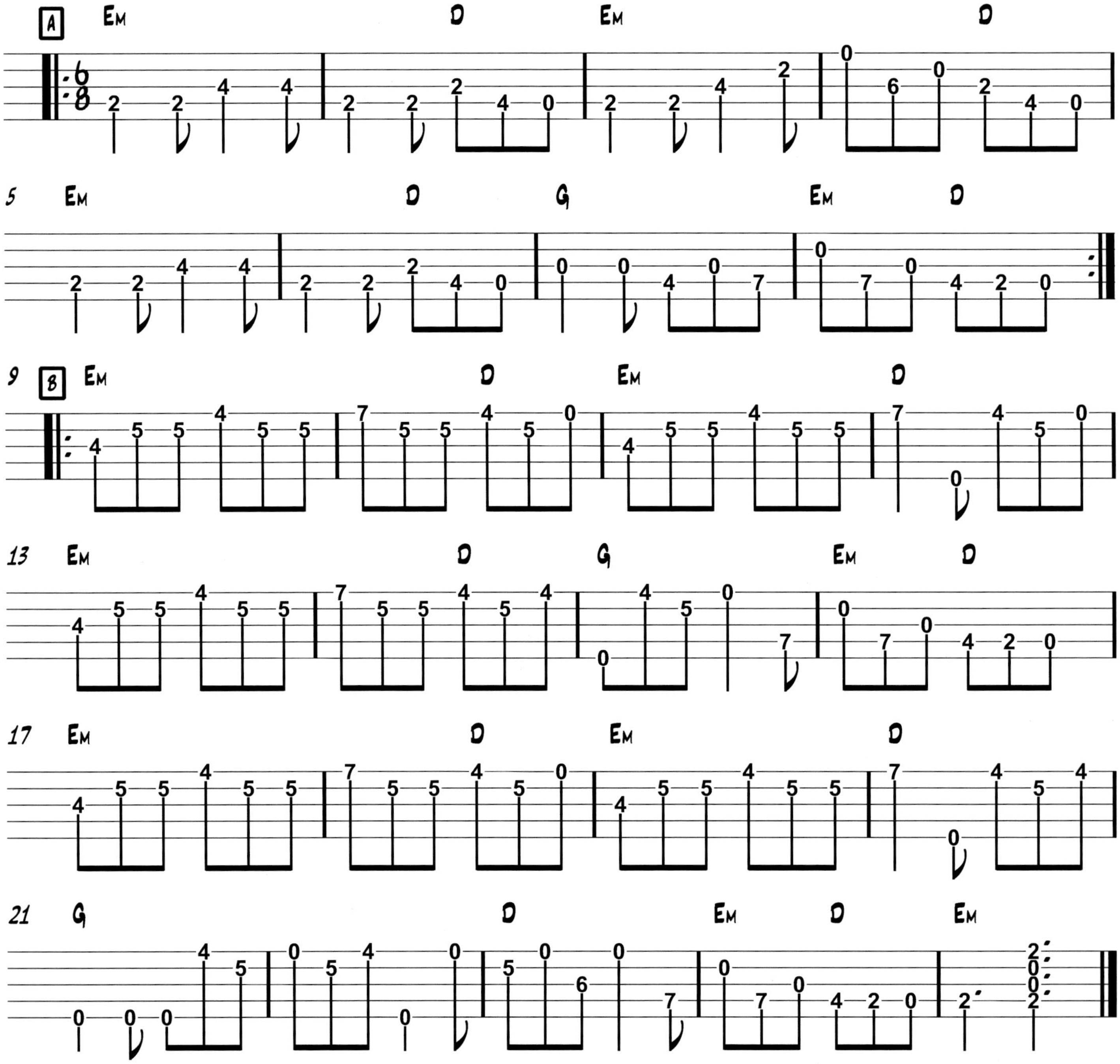

The Cuckoo

Traditional
Arr. Lluis Gómez

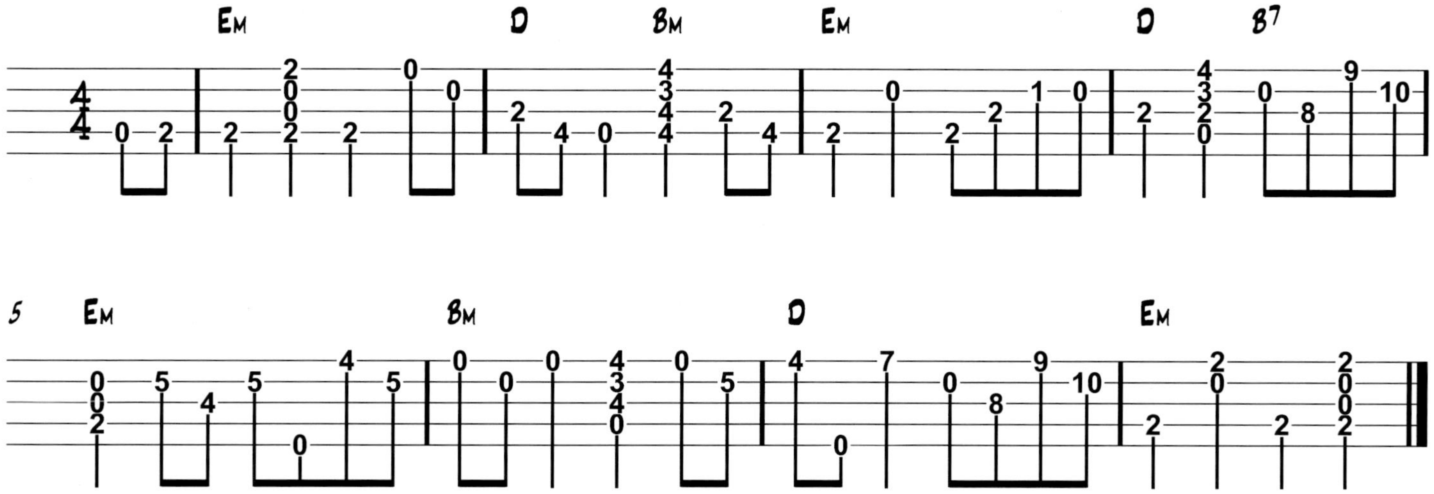

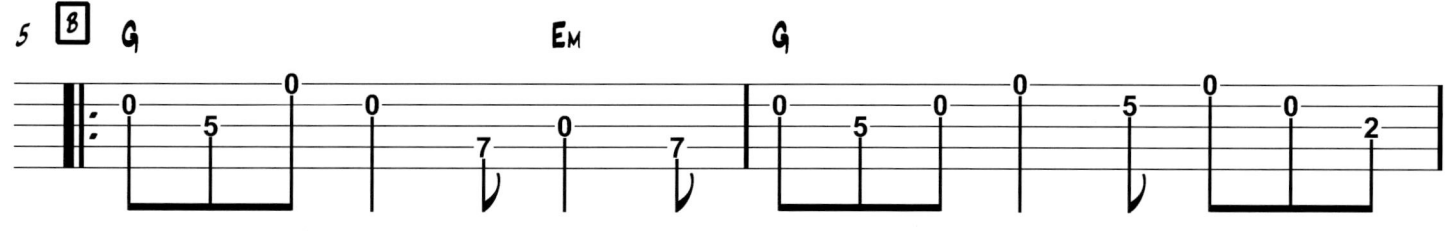

Barney's Goat

Traditional
Arr. Lluis Gómez

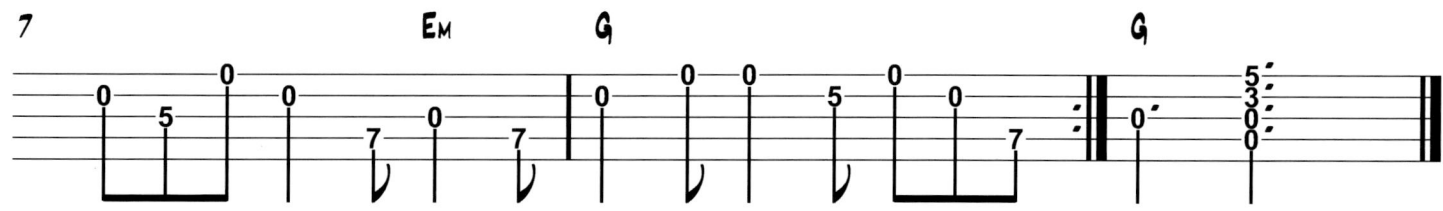

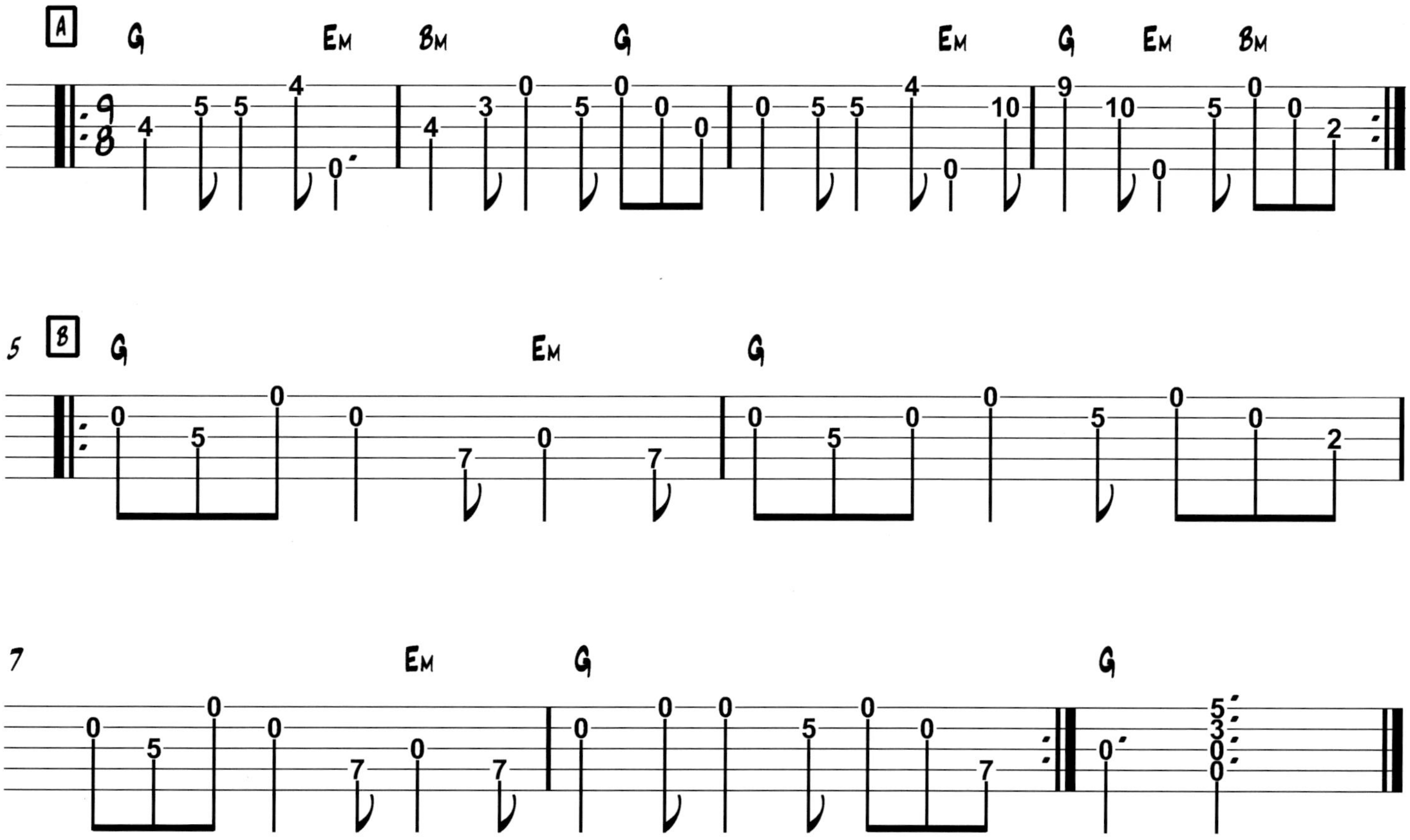

The Clergy's Lamentation

O'Carolan
Arr. Lluís Gómez

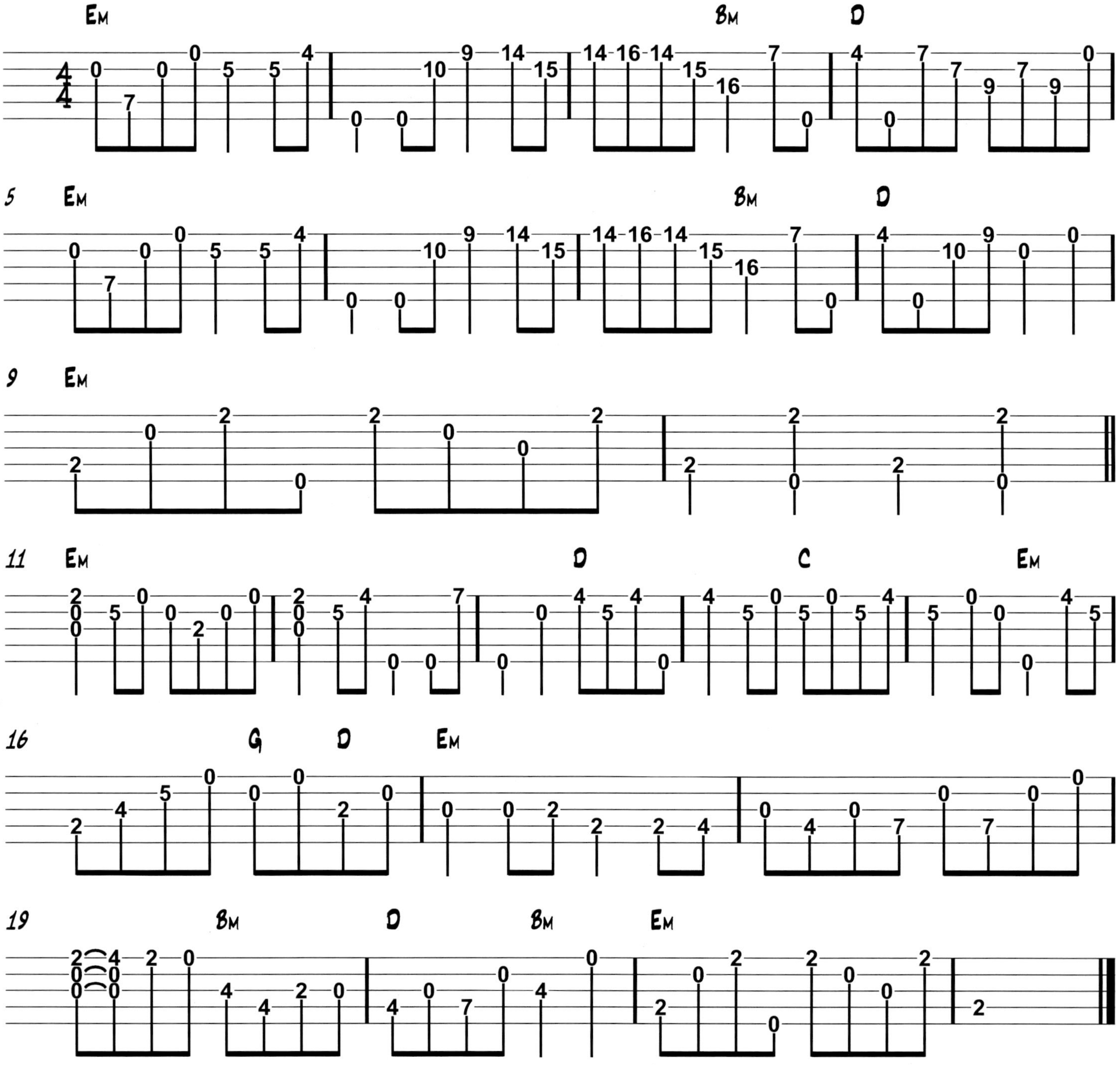

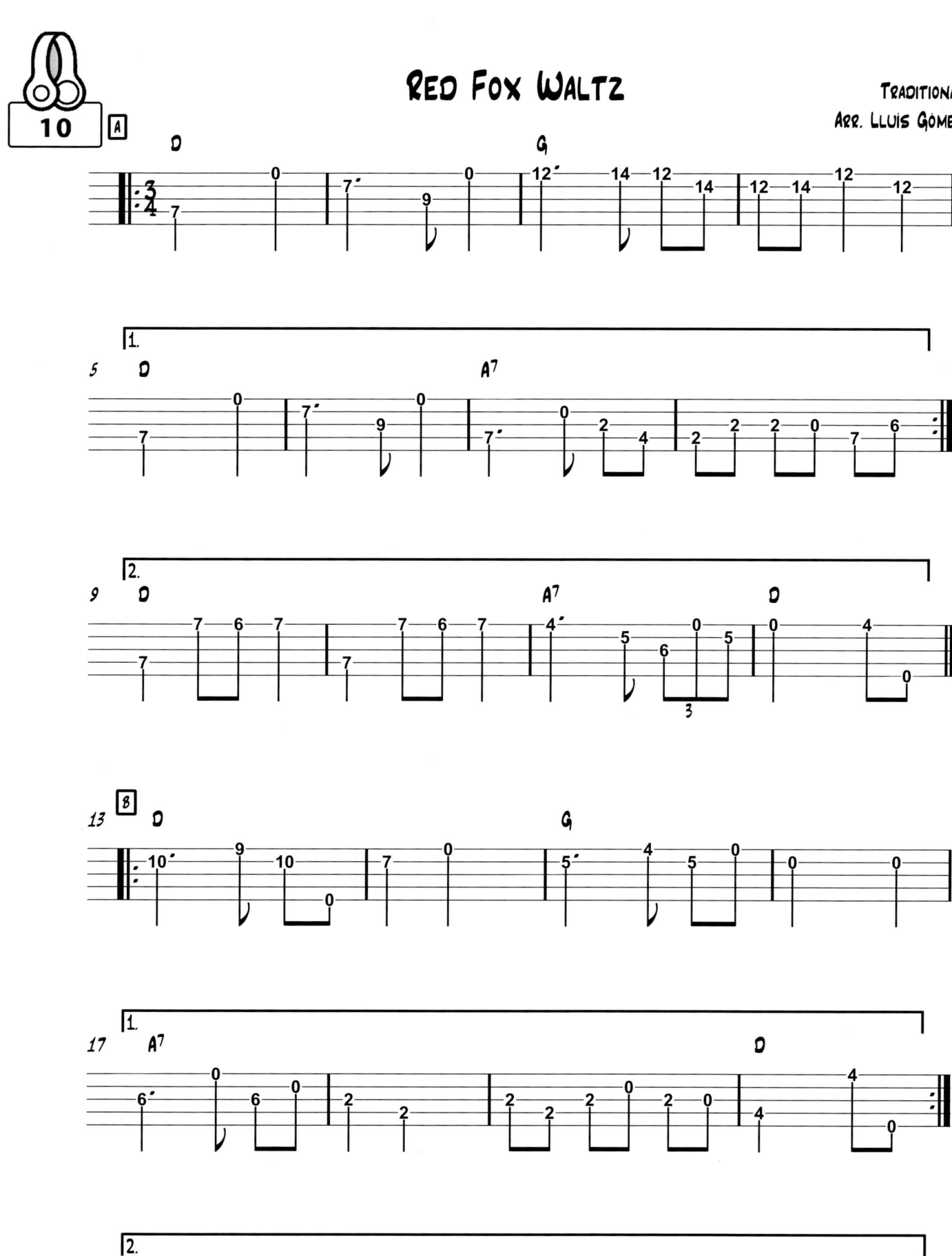

The Downfall of Paris

Traditional
Arr. Lluis Gómez

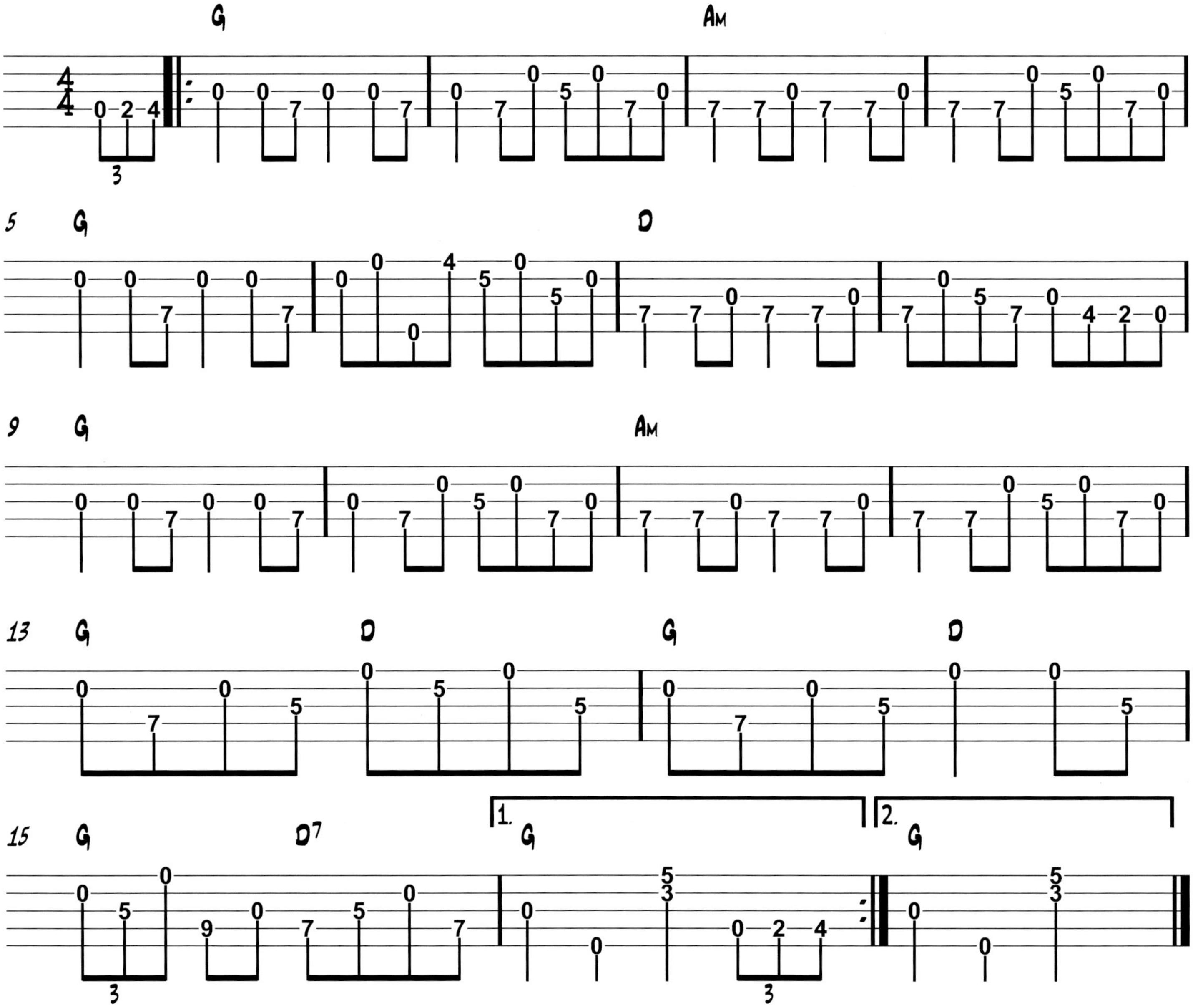

Reel de Lapin

Traditional
Arr. Lluis Gómez

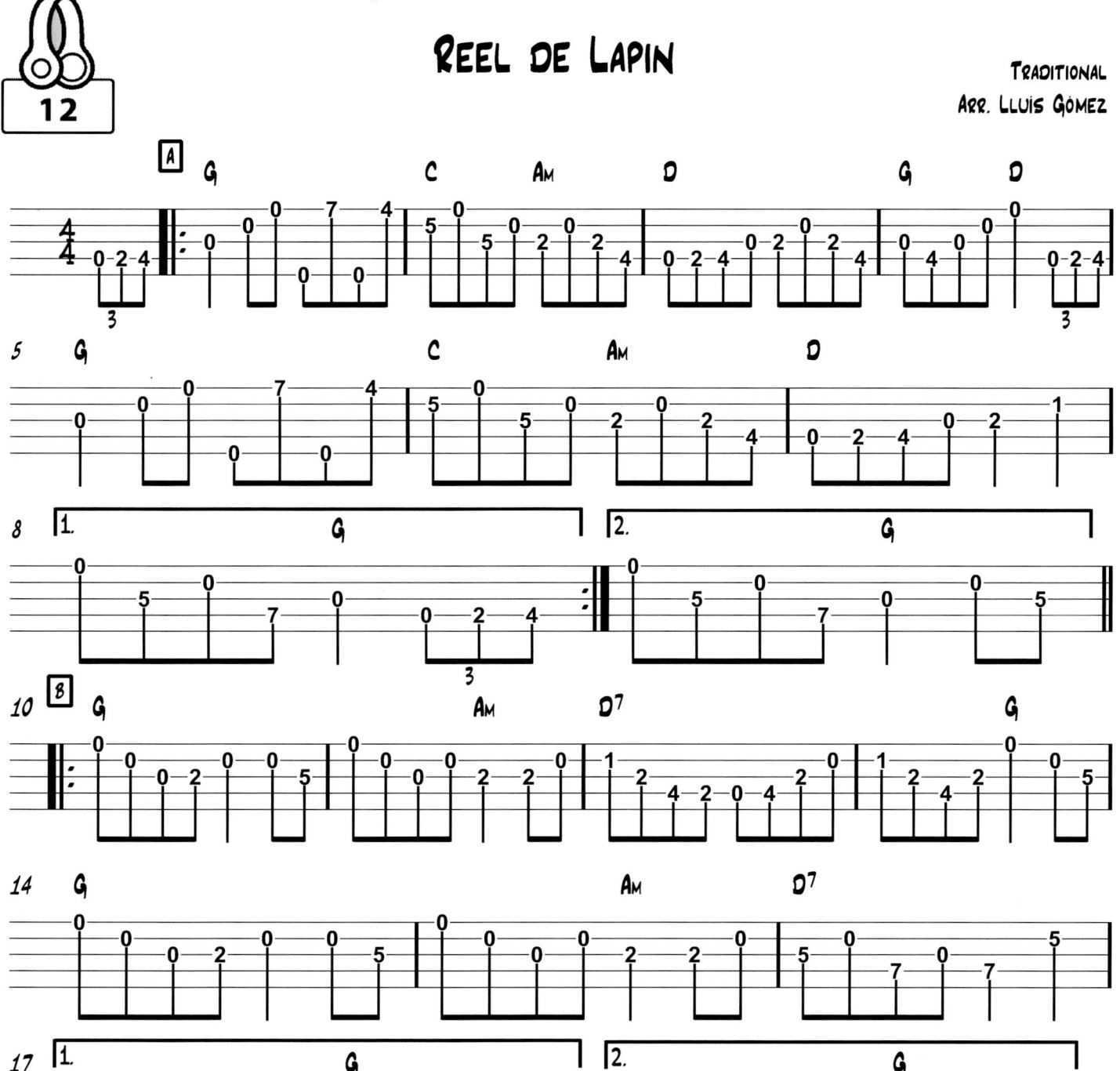

Eleven Mile Canyon

William Bay
Arr. Lluís Gómez

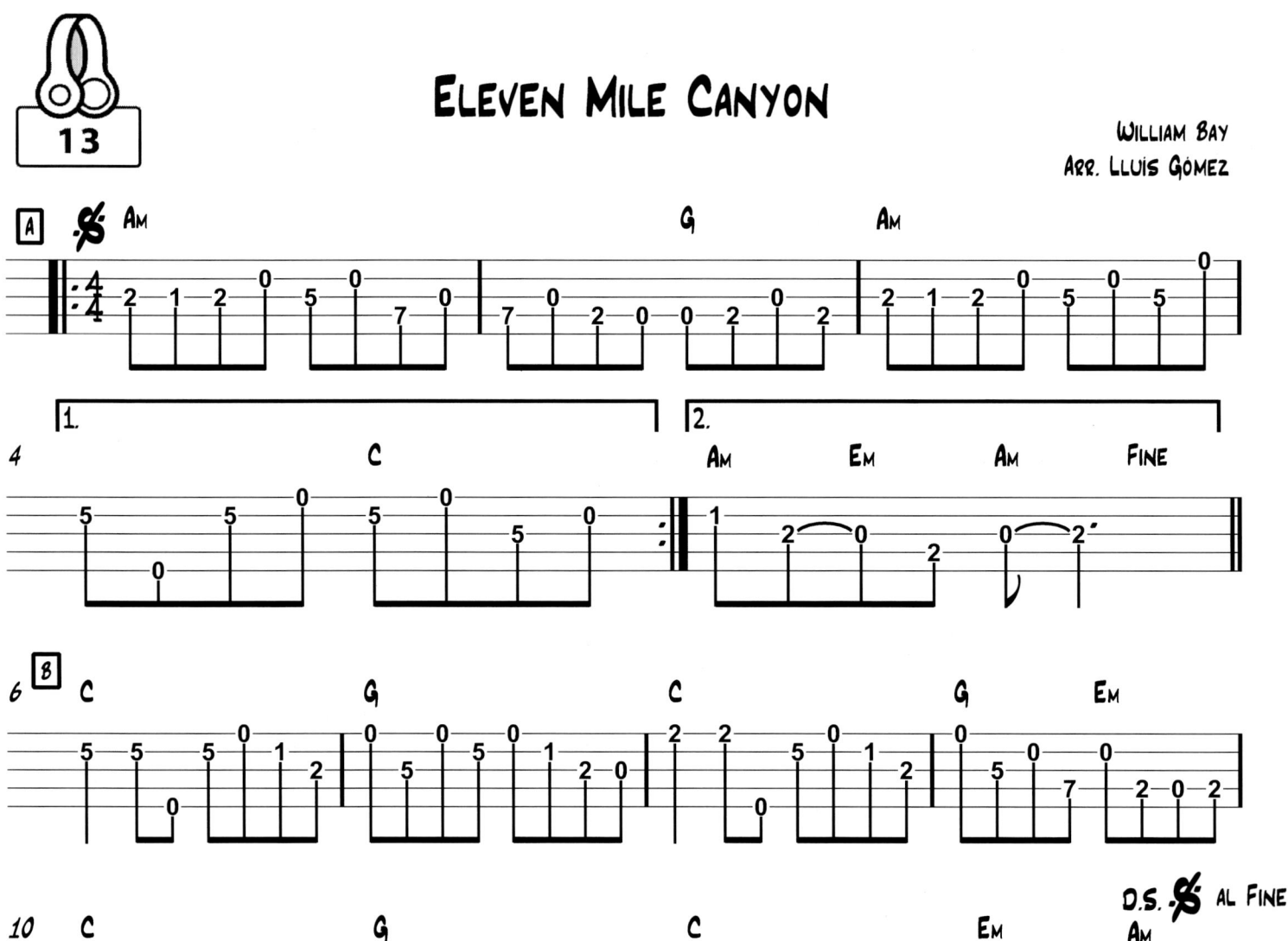

©2020 by William Bay. All rights reserved.

The Burning of the Piper's Hut

Scottish March
Arr. Lluis Gómez

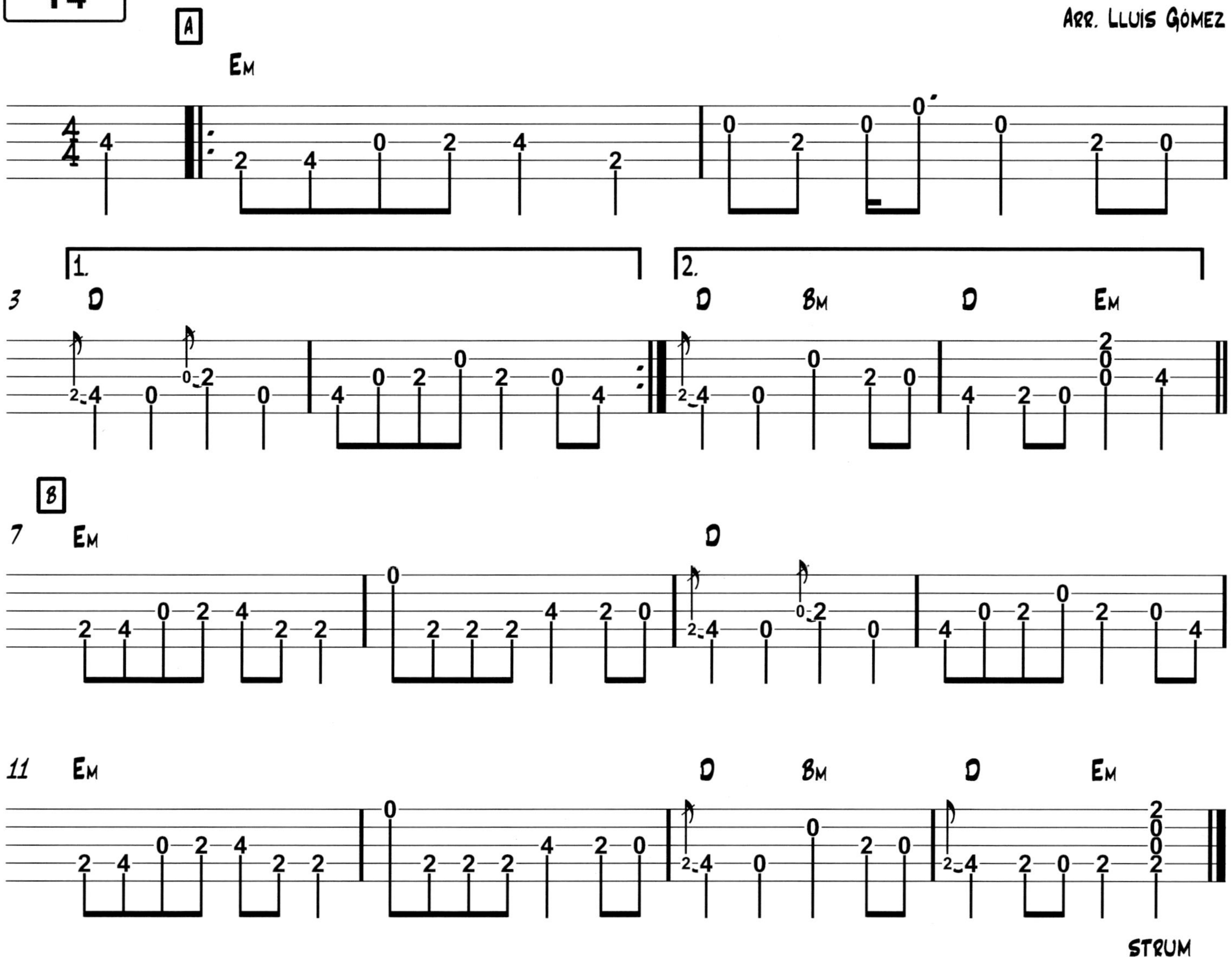

Young McGoldrick

William Bay
Arr. Lluís Gómez

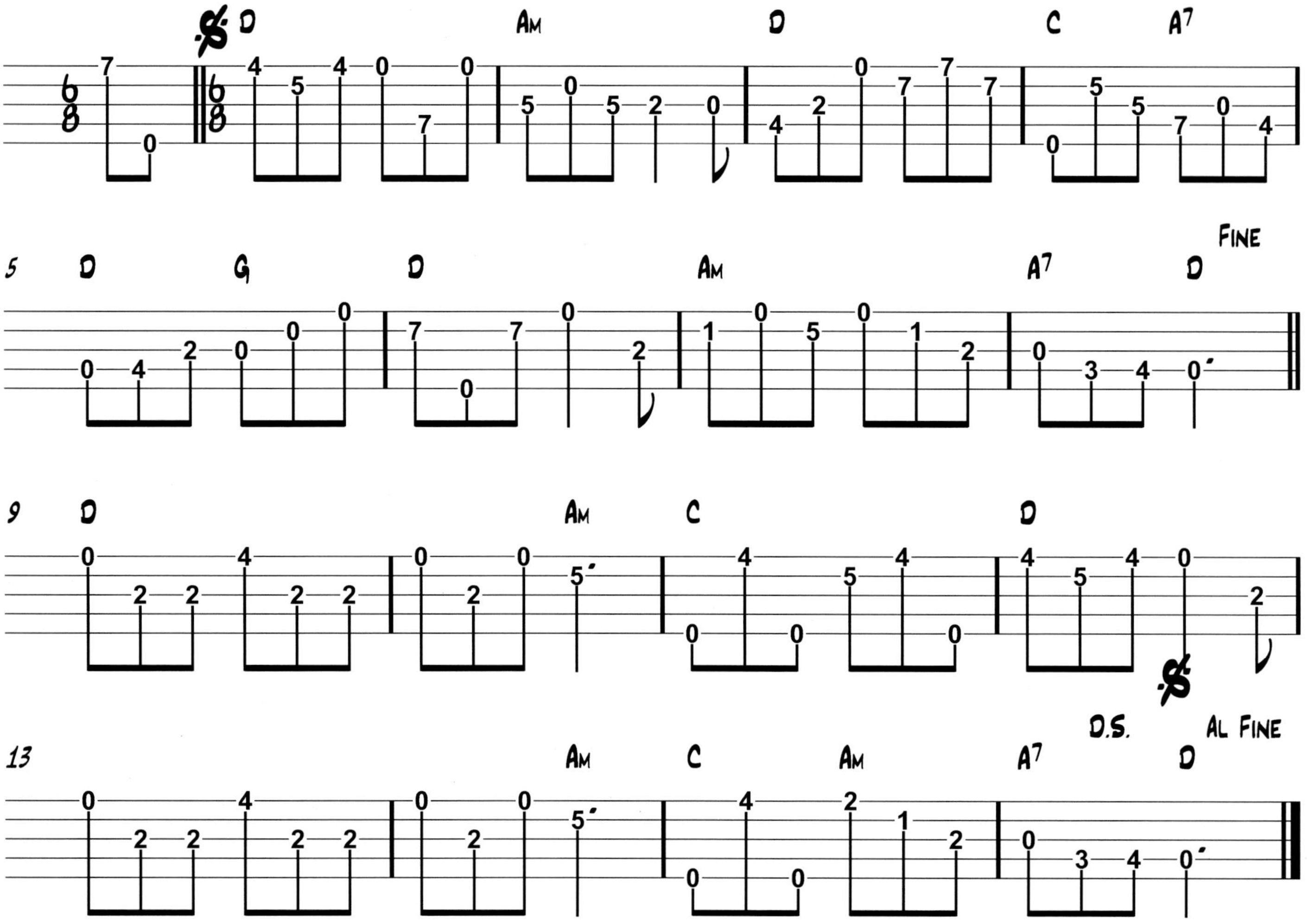

Jackson's Jig

Traditional
Arr. Lluis Gómez

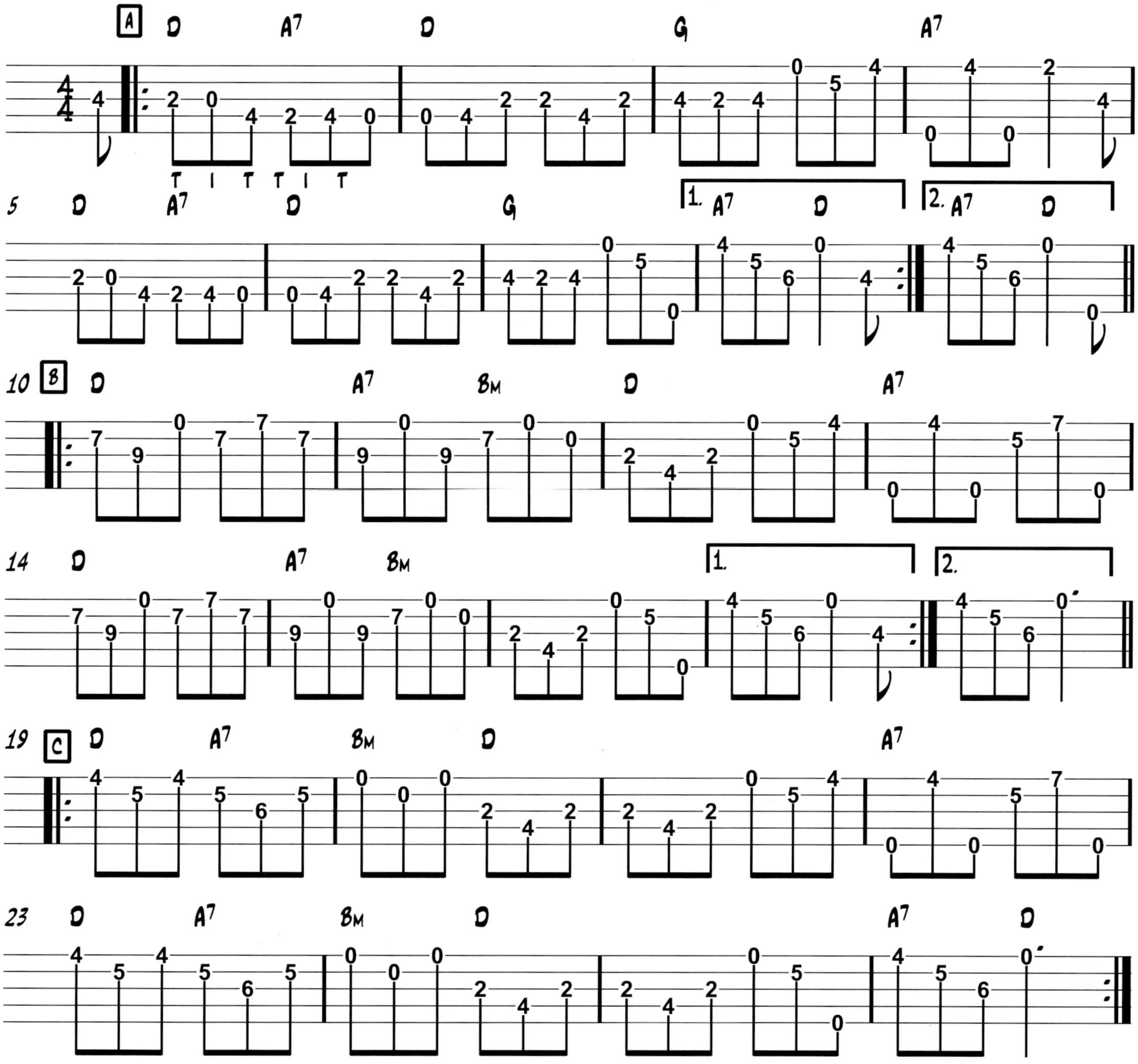

Little House 'Round the Corner

Irish Jig
Arr. Lluís Gómez

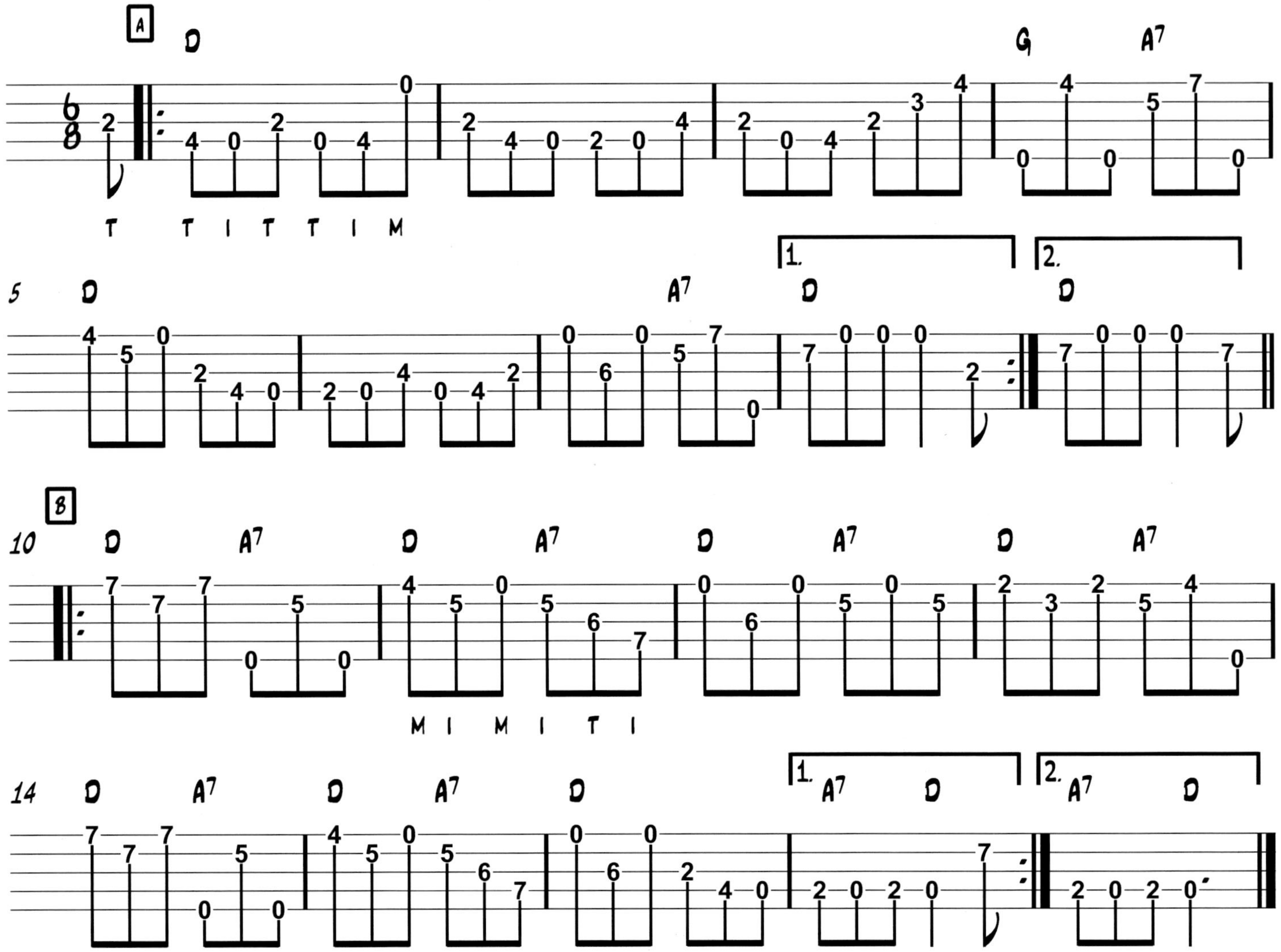

Missouri Mud

Fiddle Tune
Arr. Lluis Gómez

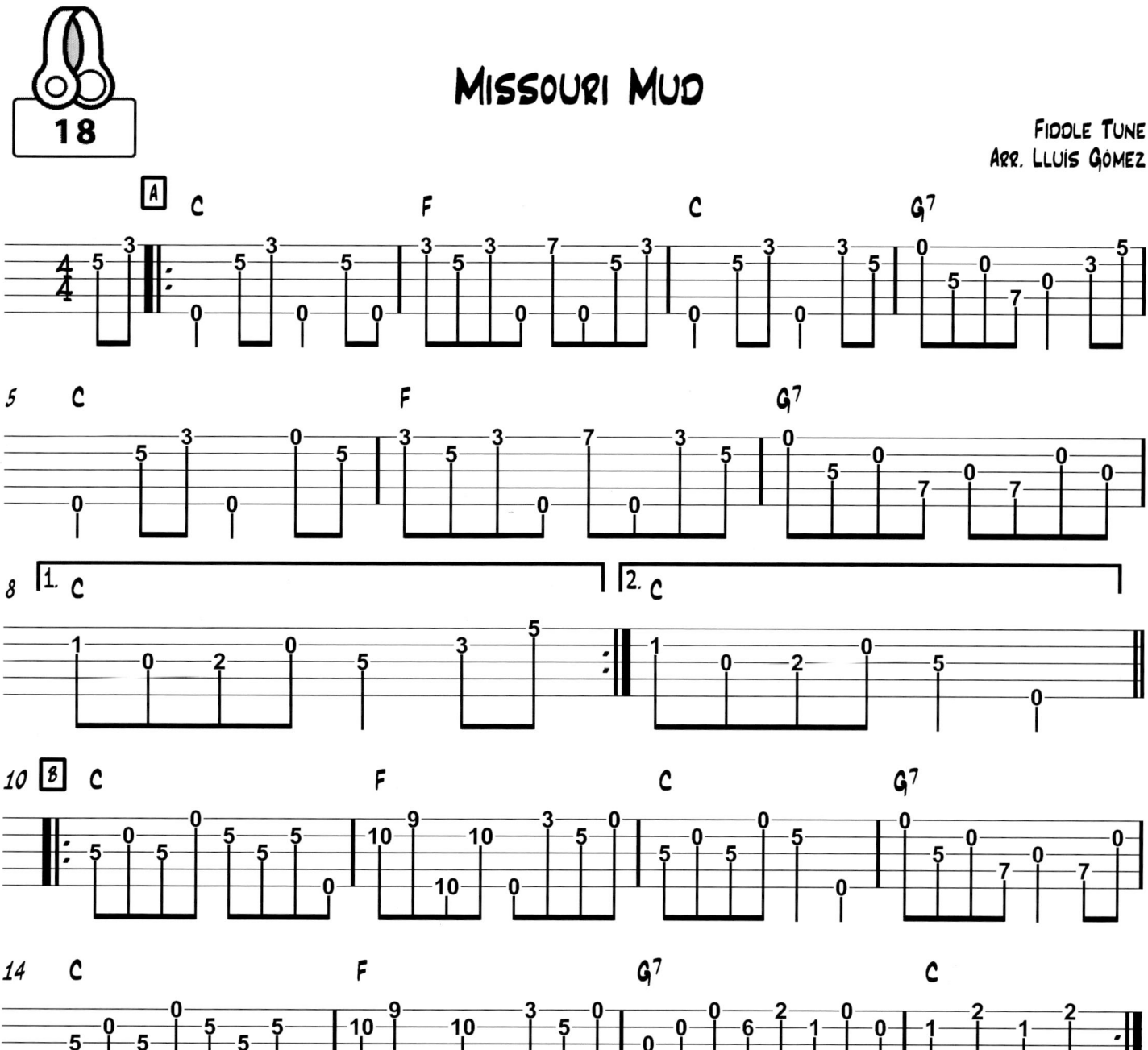

Whiskey Before Breakfast

Traditional
Arr. Lluís Gómez

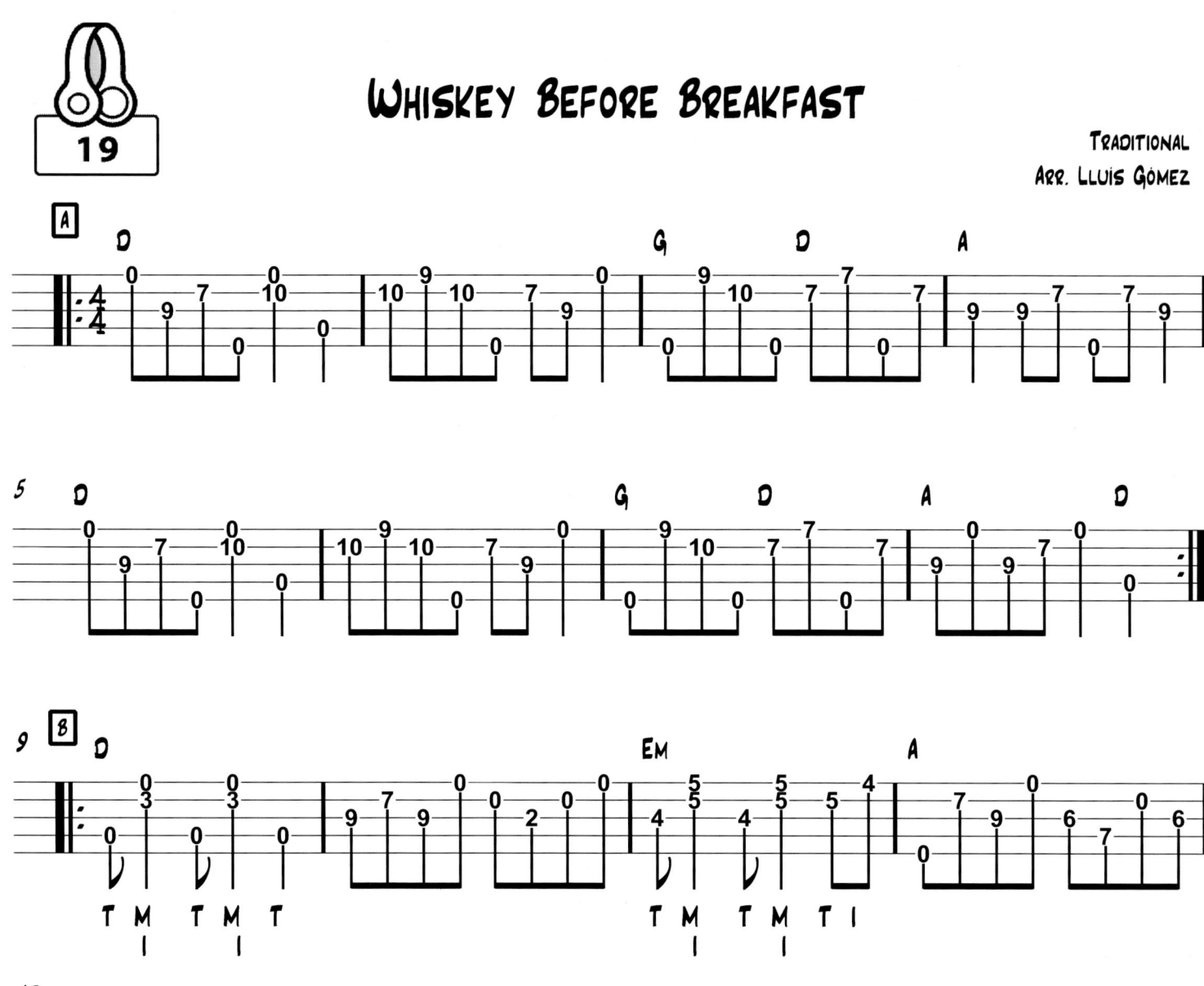

Neapolitan Threshers

Traditional
Arr. Lluís Gómez

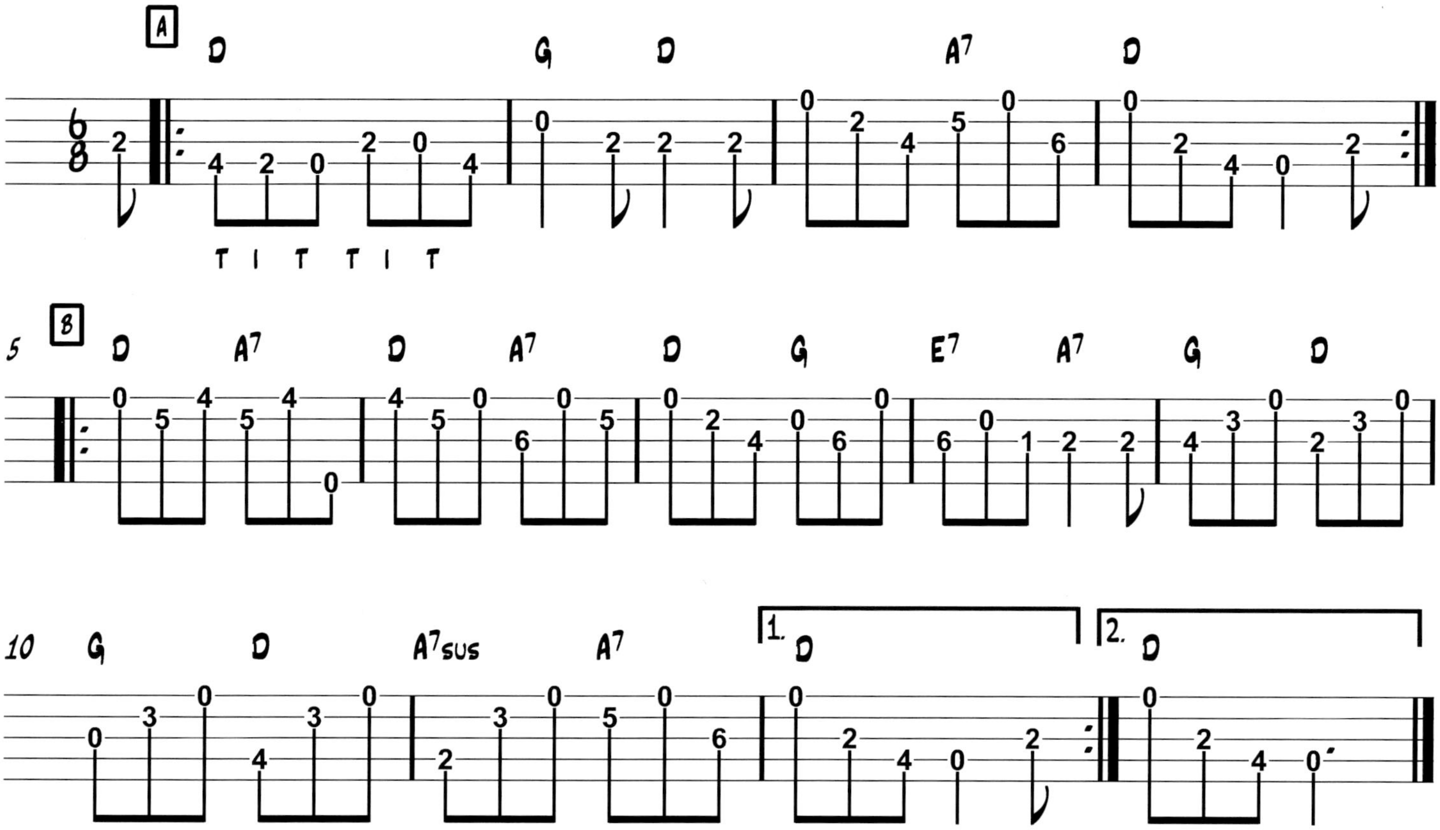

The Eighth of January

Traditional
Arr. Lluis Gómez

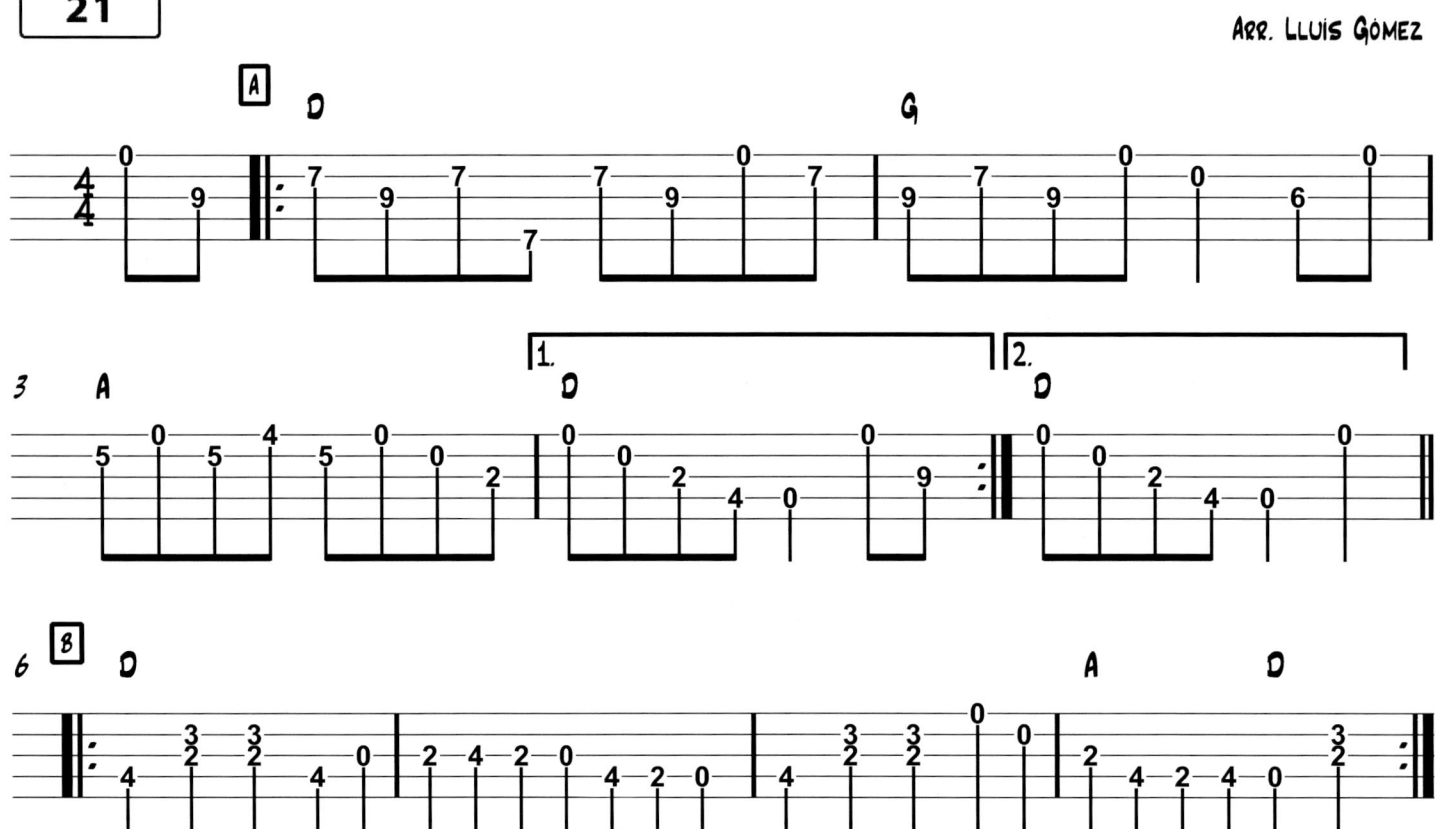

Harvest Moon Strathspey

Traditional
Arr. Lluis Gómez

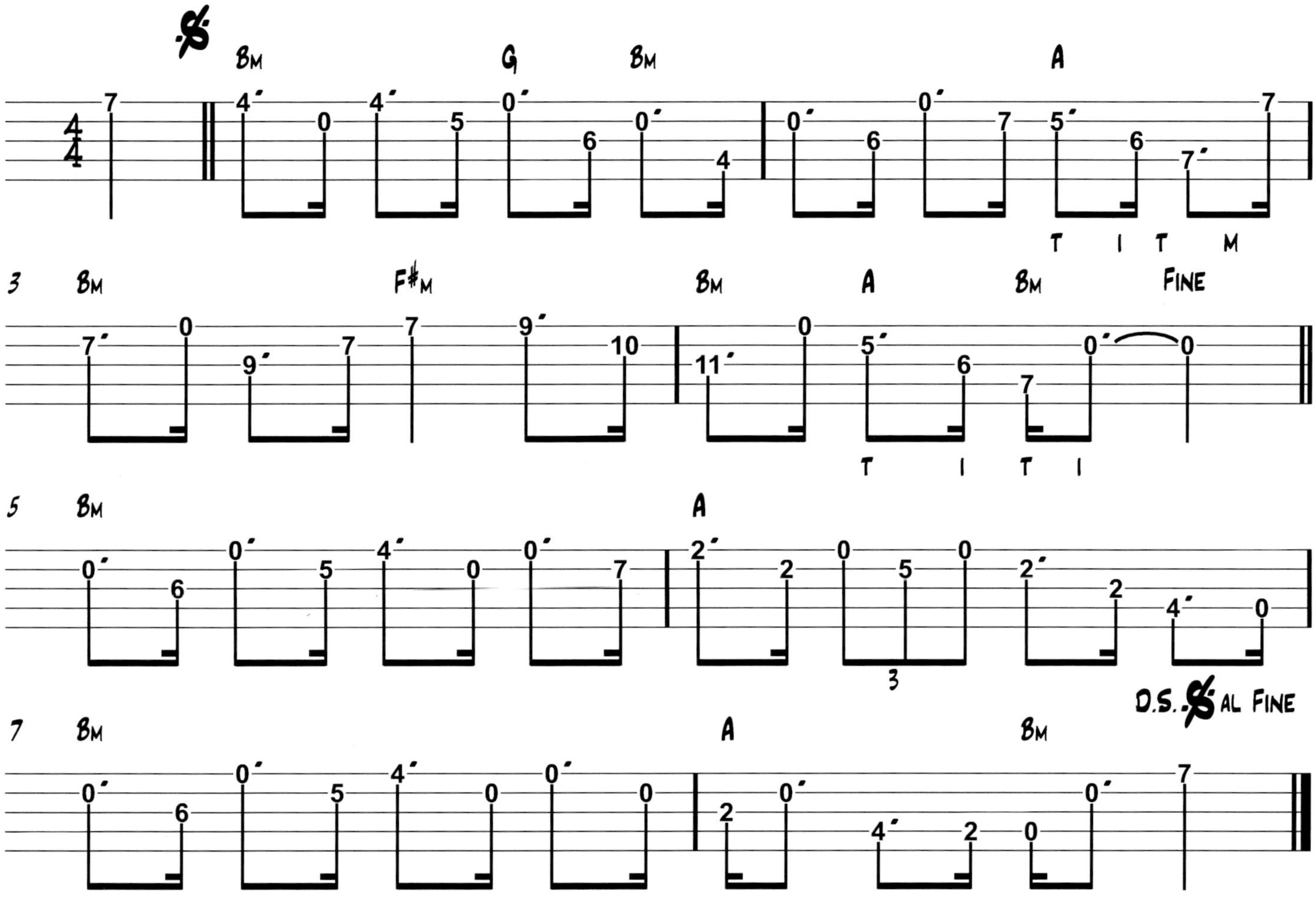

Buttermilk Jig

Traditional
Arr. Lluís Gómez

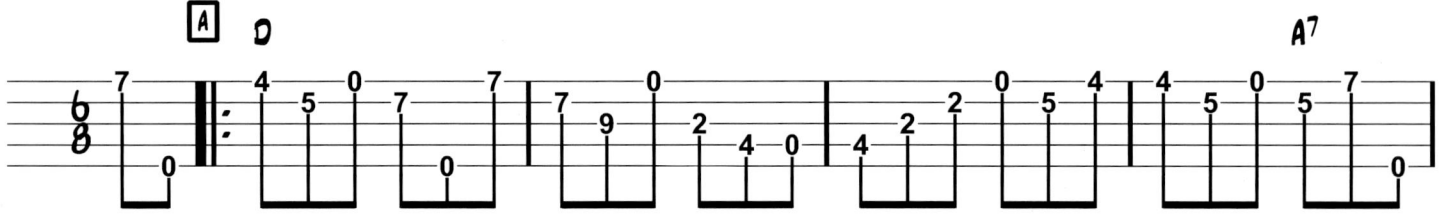
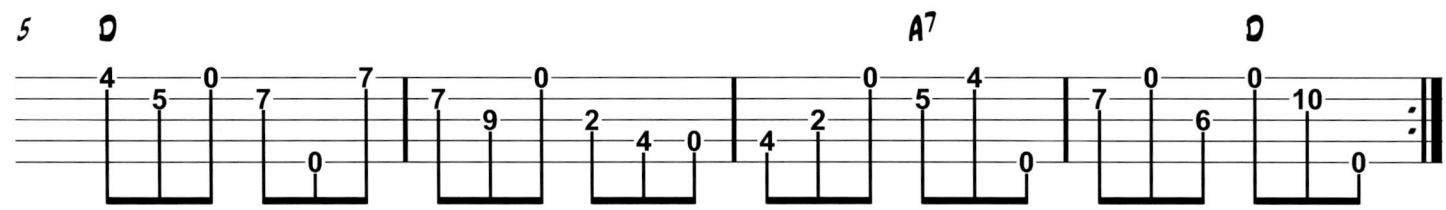
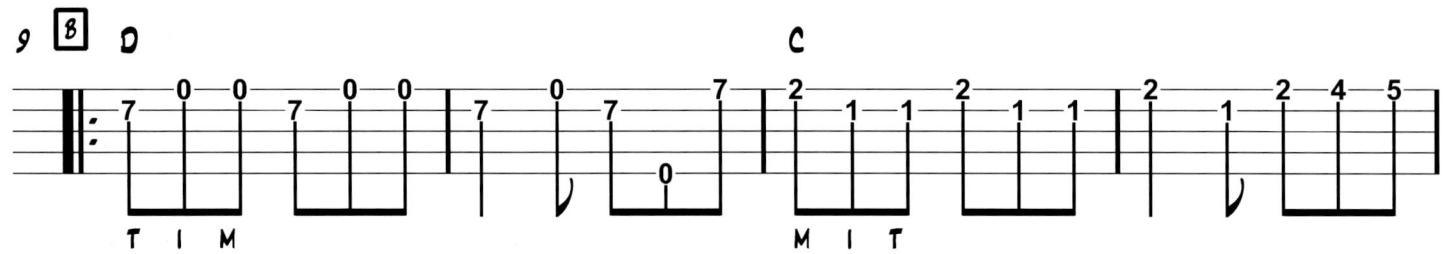
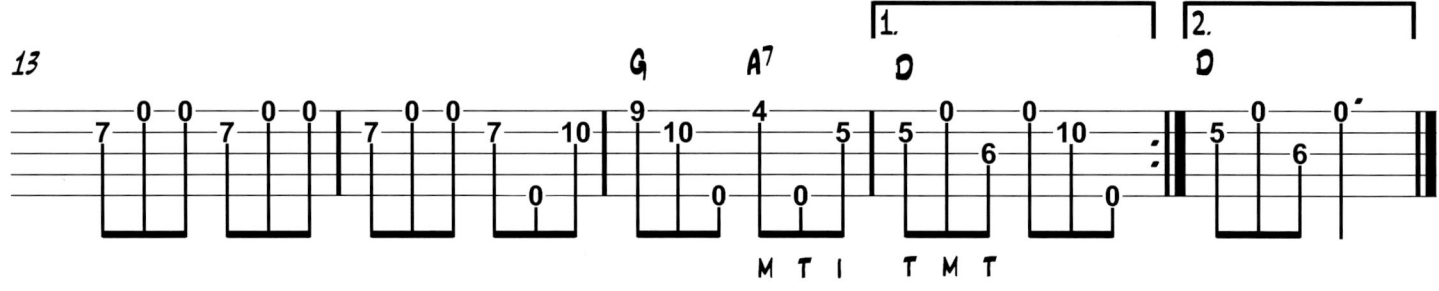

An Comhra Donn

Hornpipe
Arr. Lluis Gómez

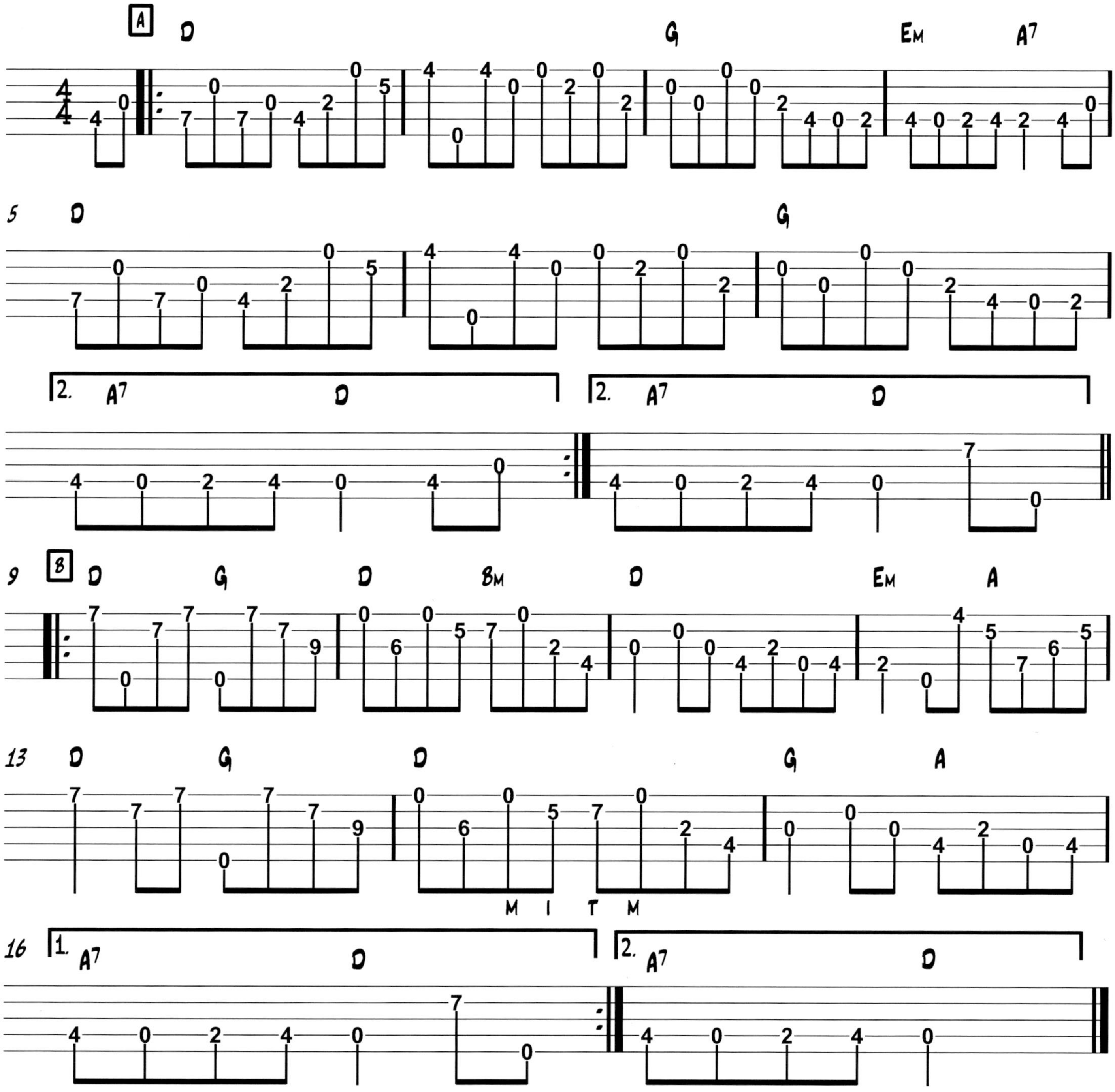

National Lancer's Hornpipe

Traditional
Arr. Lluis Gómez

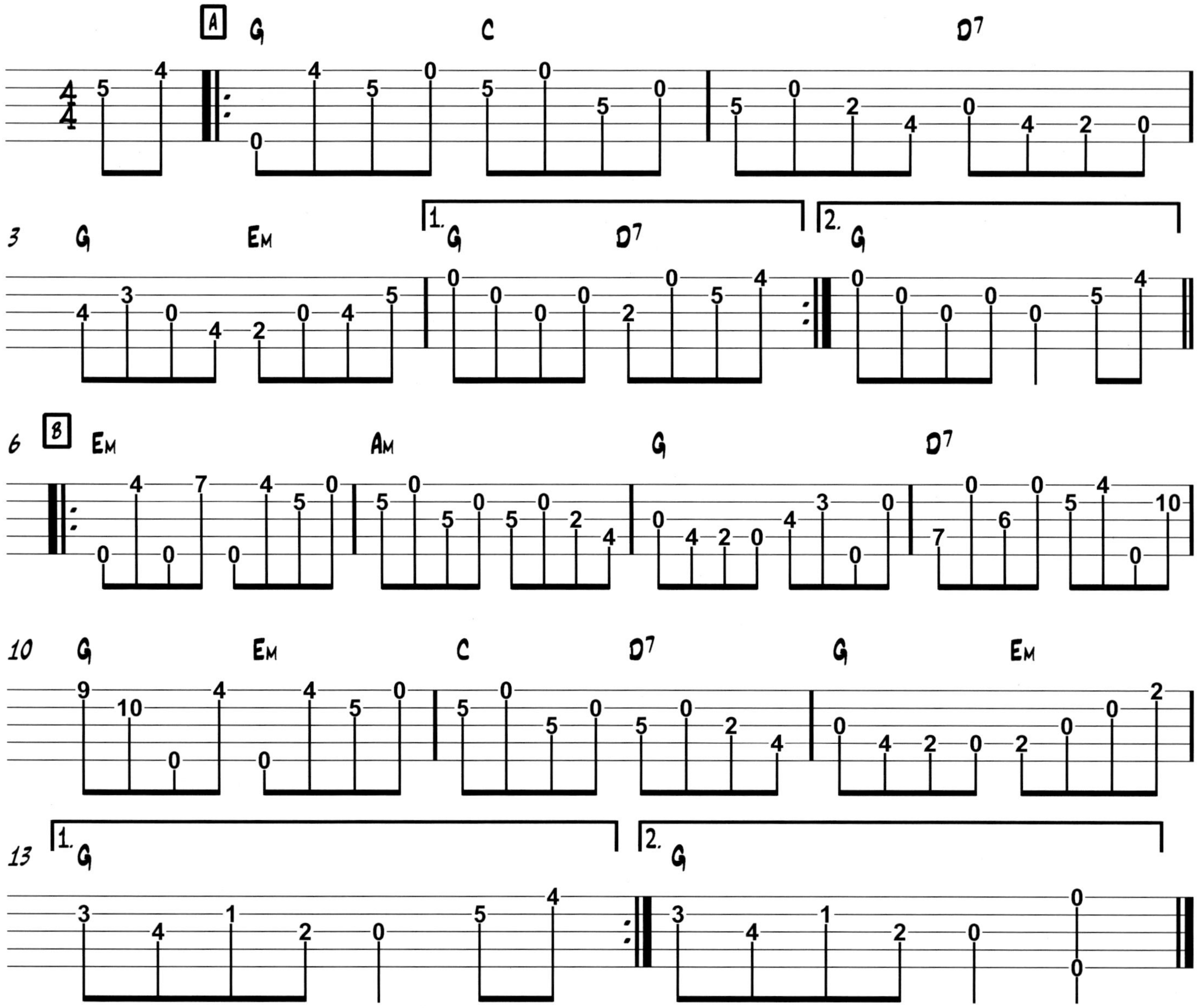

Brighton Beach

William Bay
Arr. Lluis Gómez

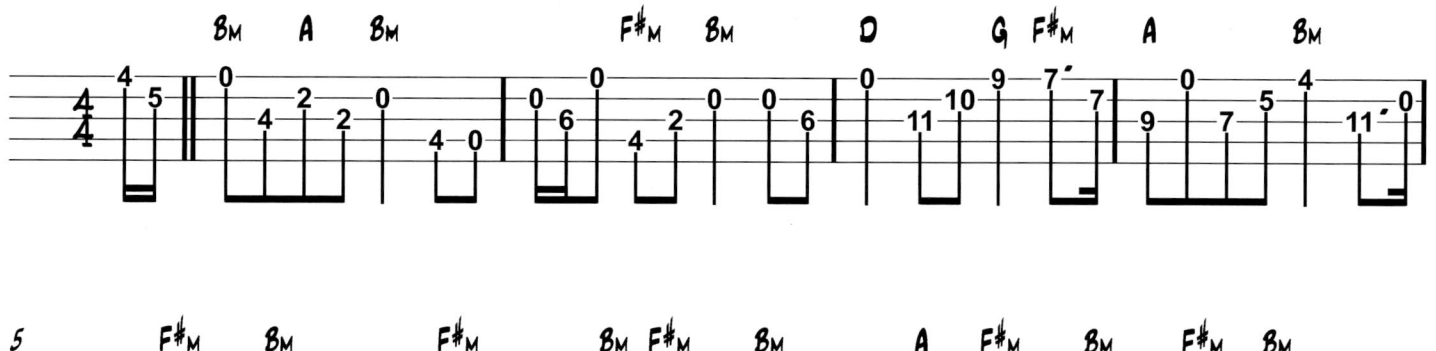

© 2020 by William Bay. All Rights Reserved.

Green Fields of America

Traditional
Arr. Lluís Gómez

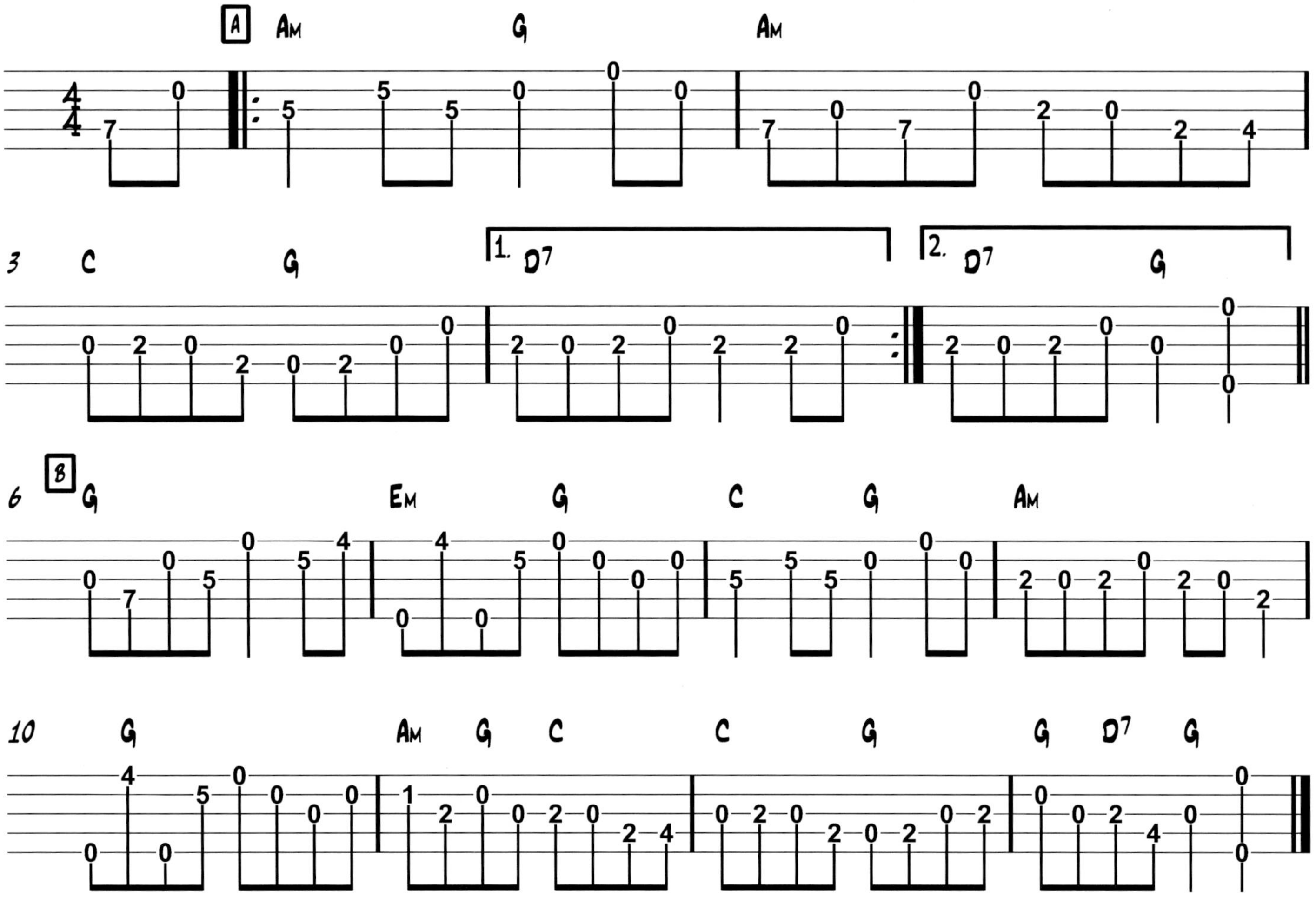

St. Clair's Hornpipe

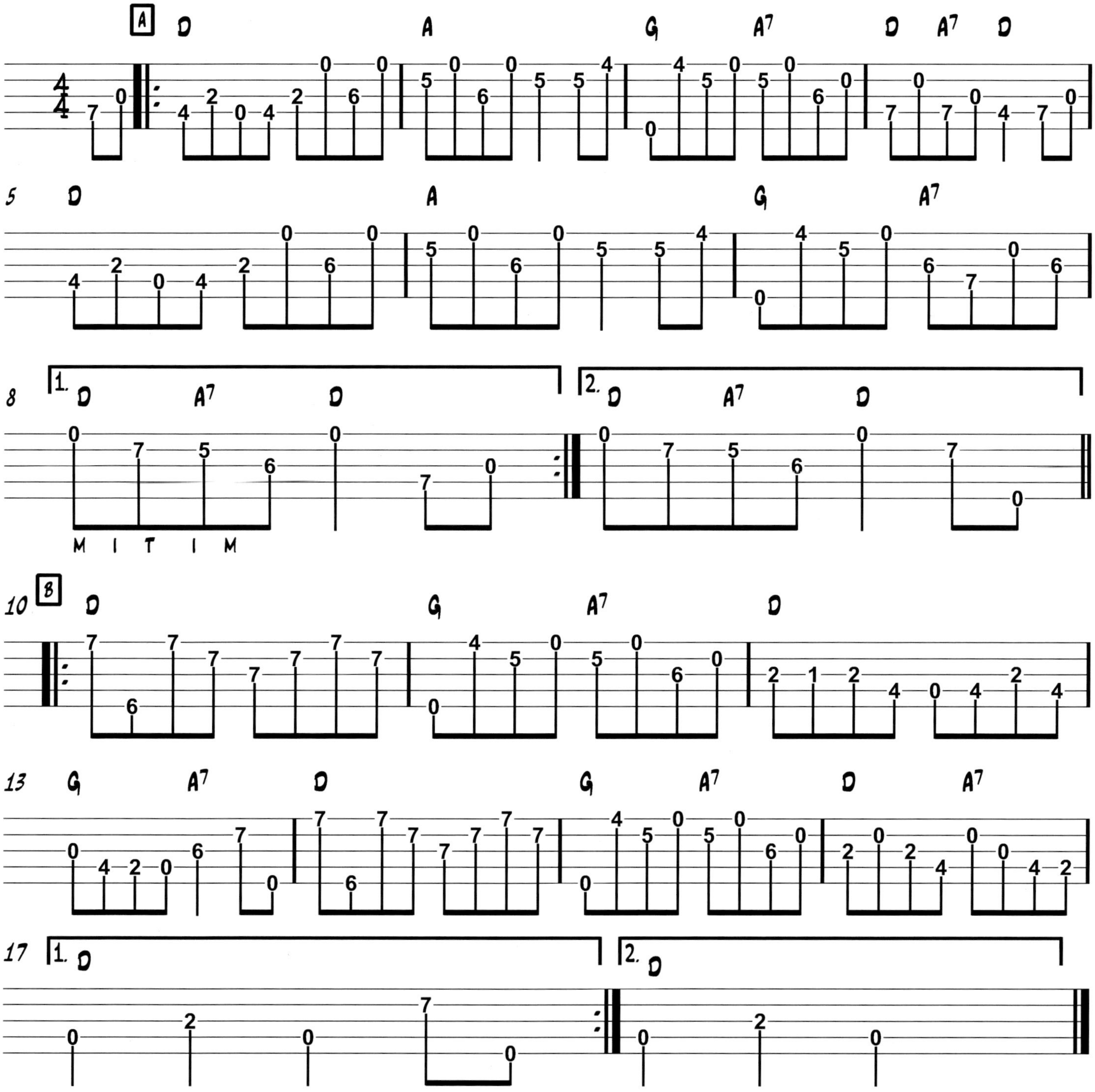

Star of Bethlehem

Traditional
Arr. Lluís Gómez

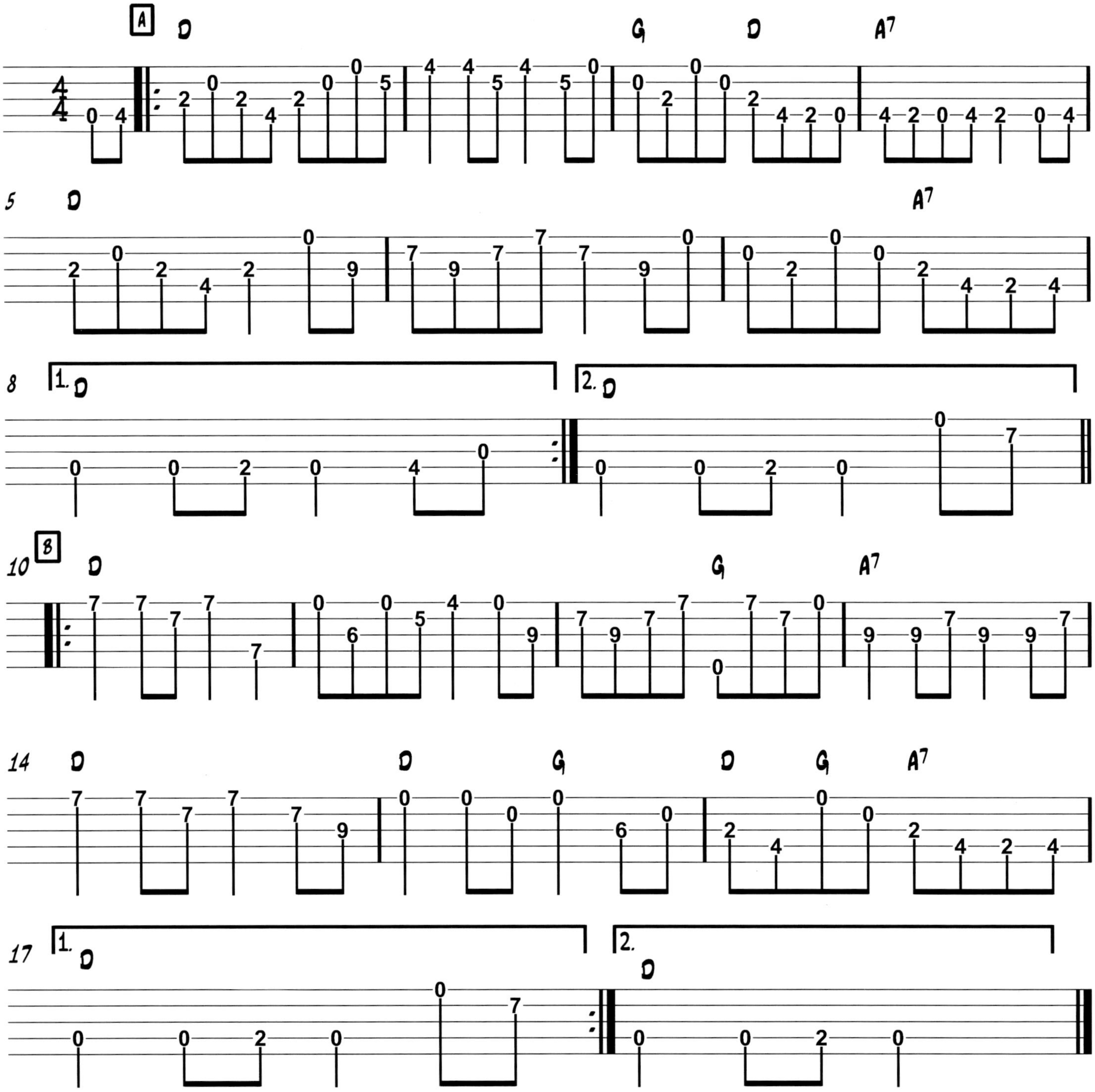

Bennett's Favorite Reel

Traditional
Arr. Lluis Gómez

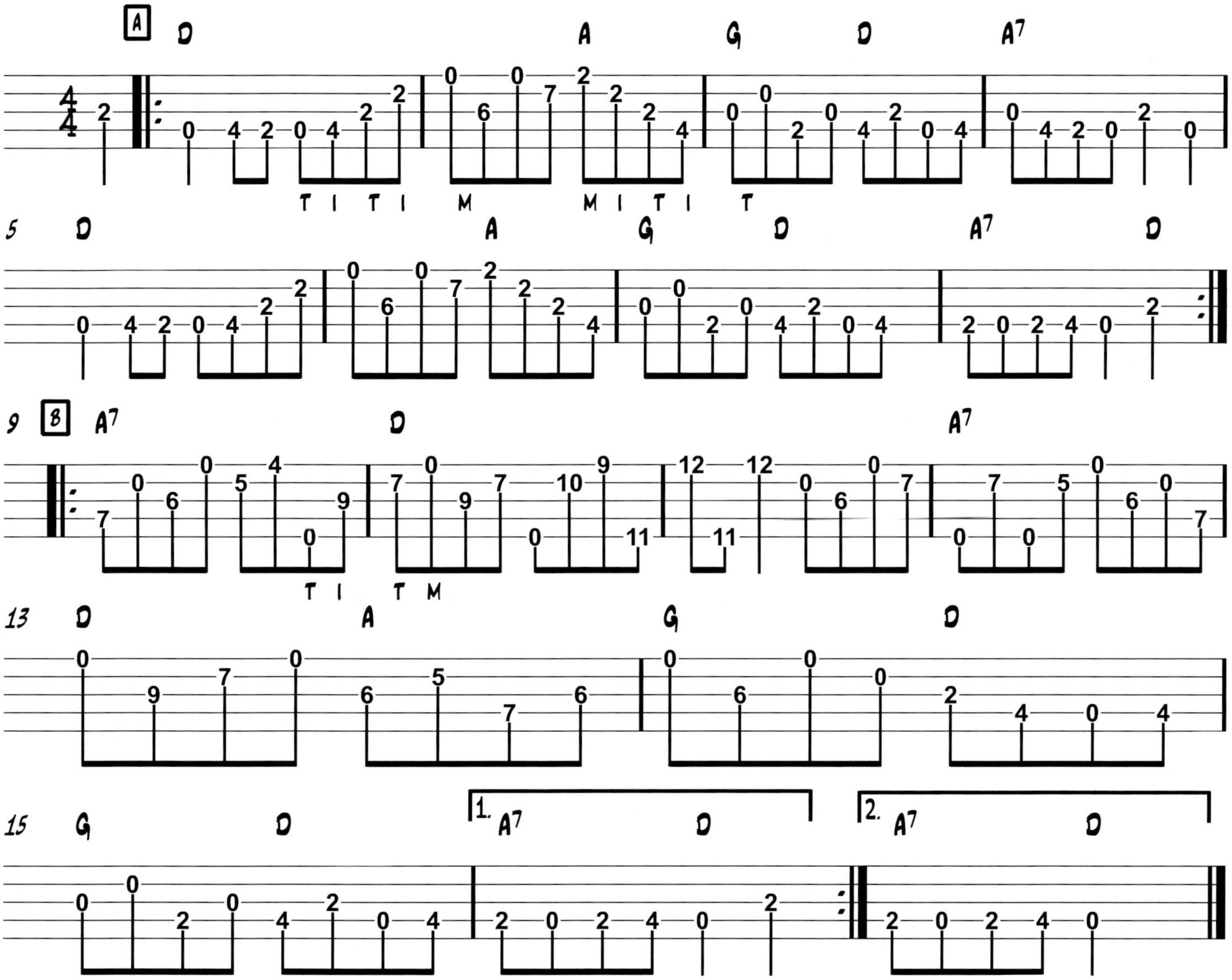

Ivy Leaf Reel

Traditional
Arr. Lluís Gómez

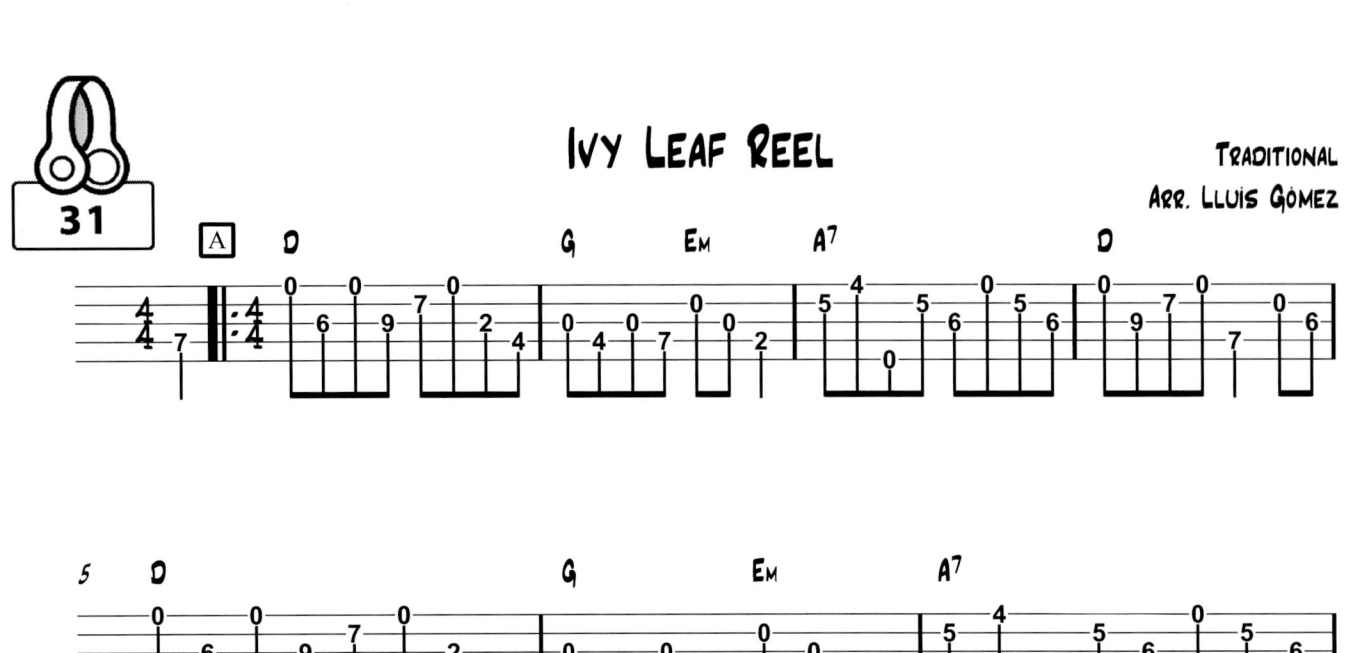
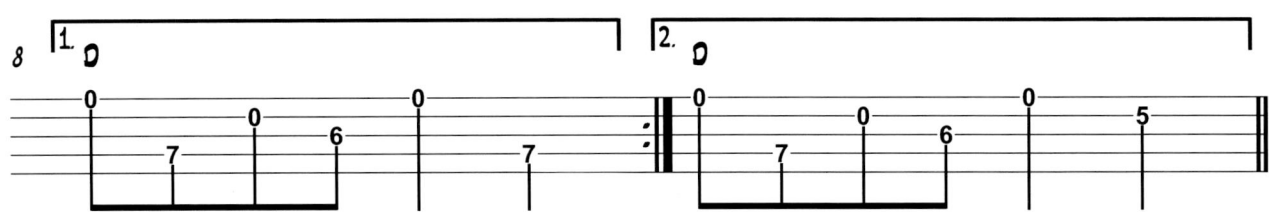
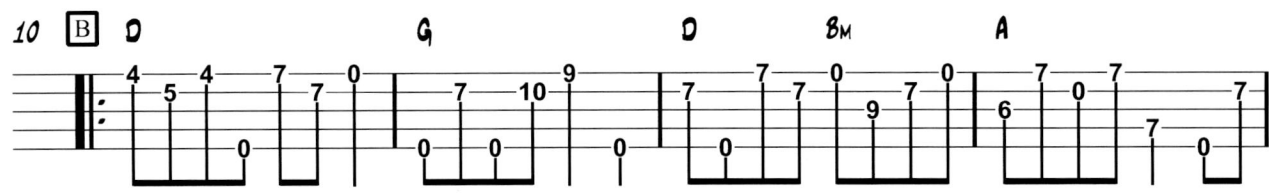
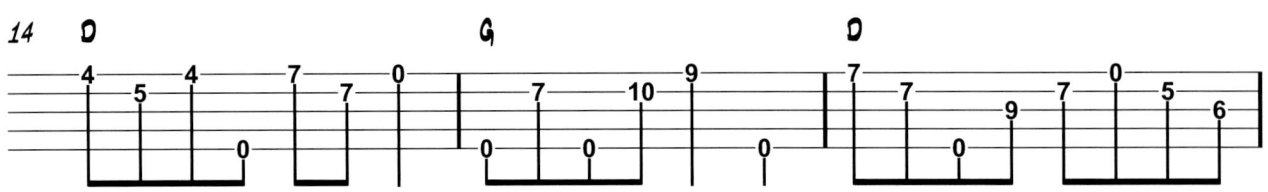
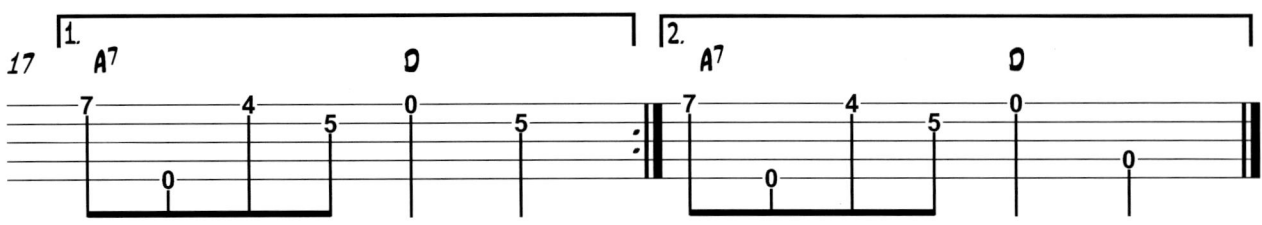

St. Anne's Reel

Traditional
Arr. Lluís Gómez

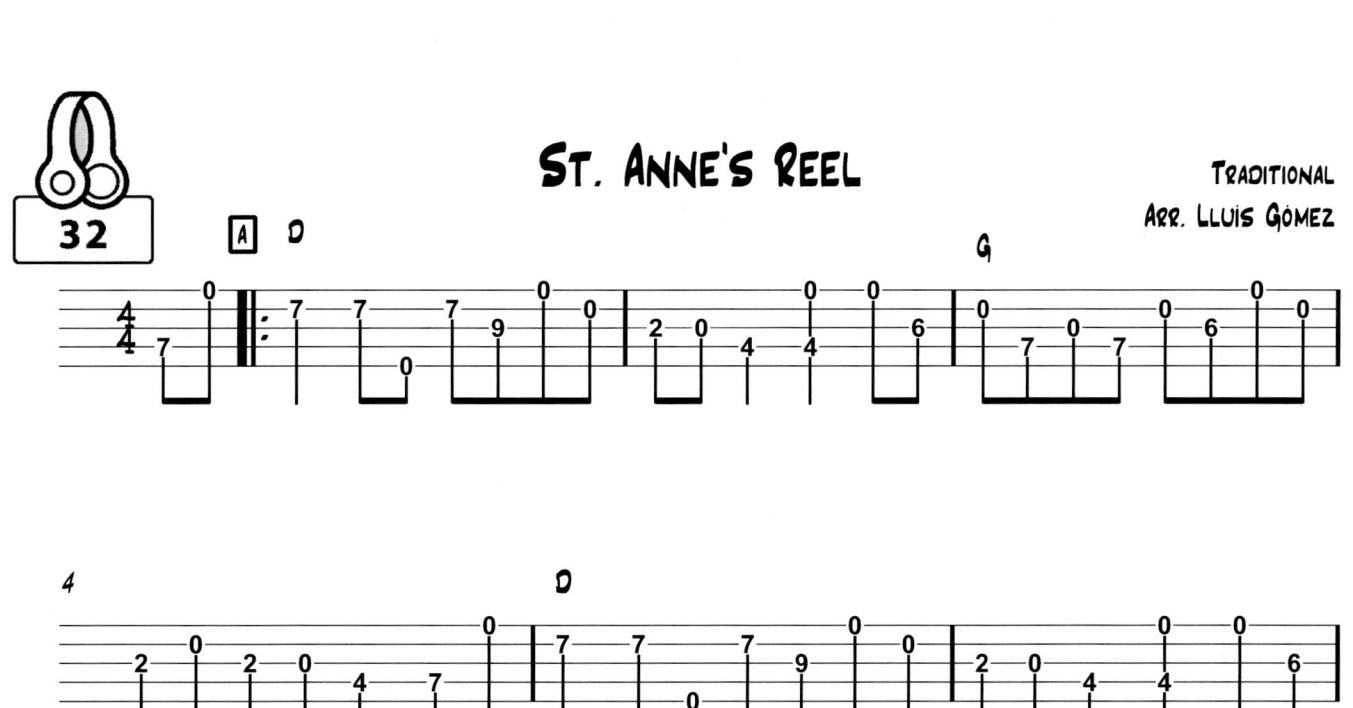
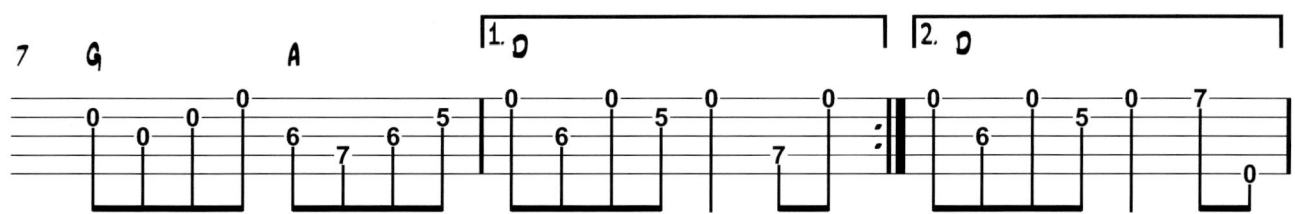
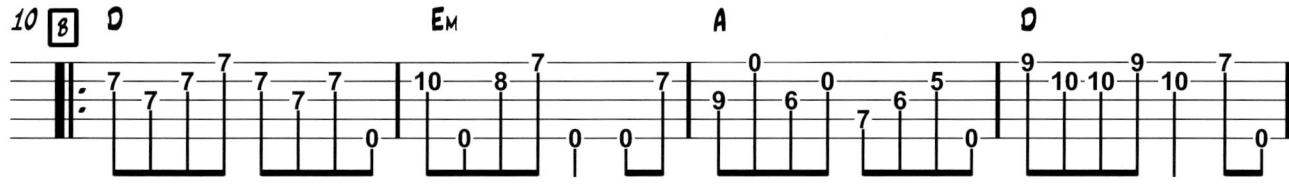
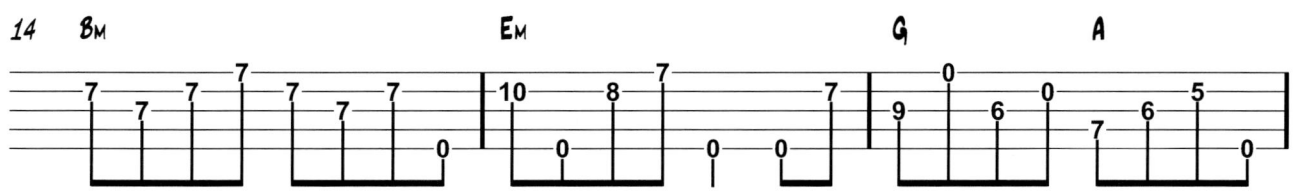
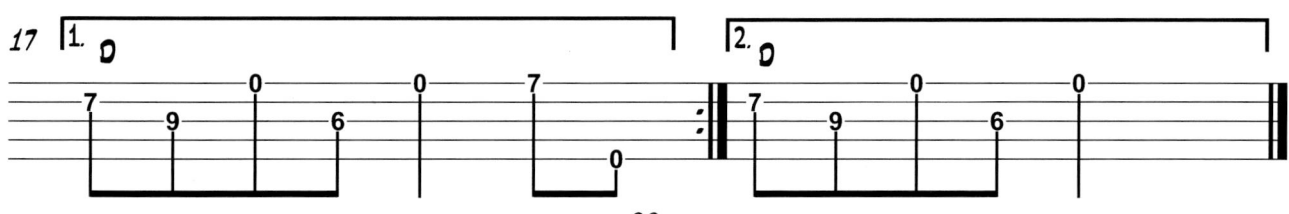

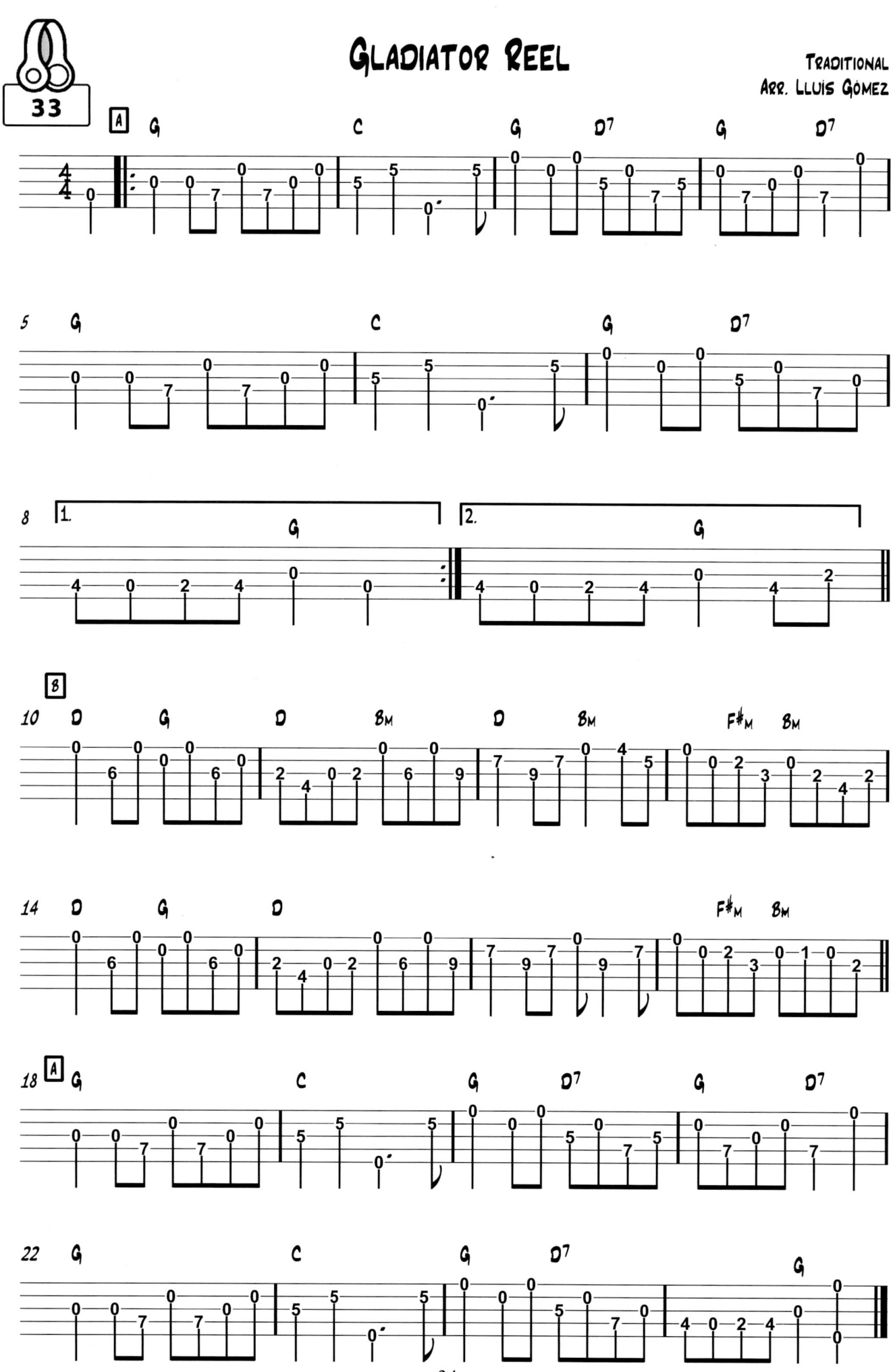

Luckie Bawdin's Reel

Scottish
Arr. Lluis Gómez

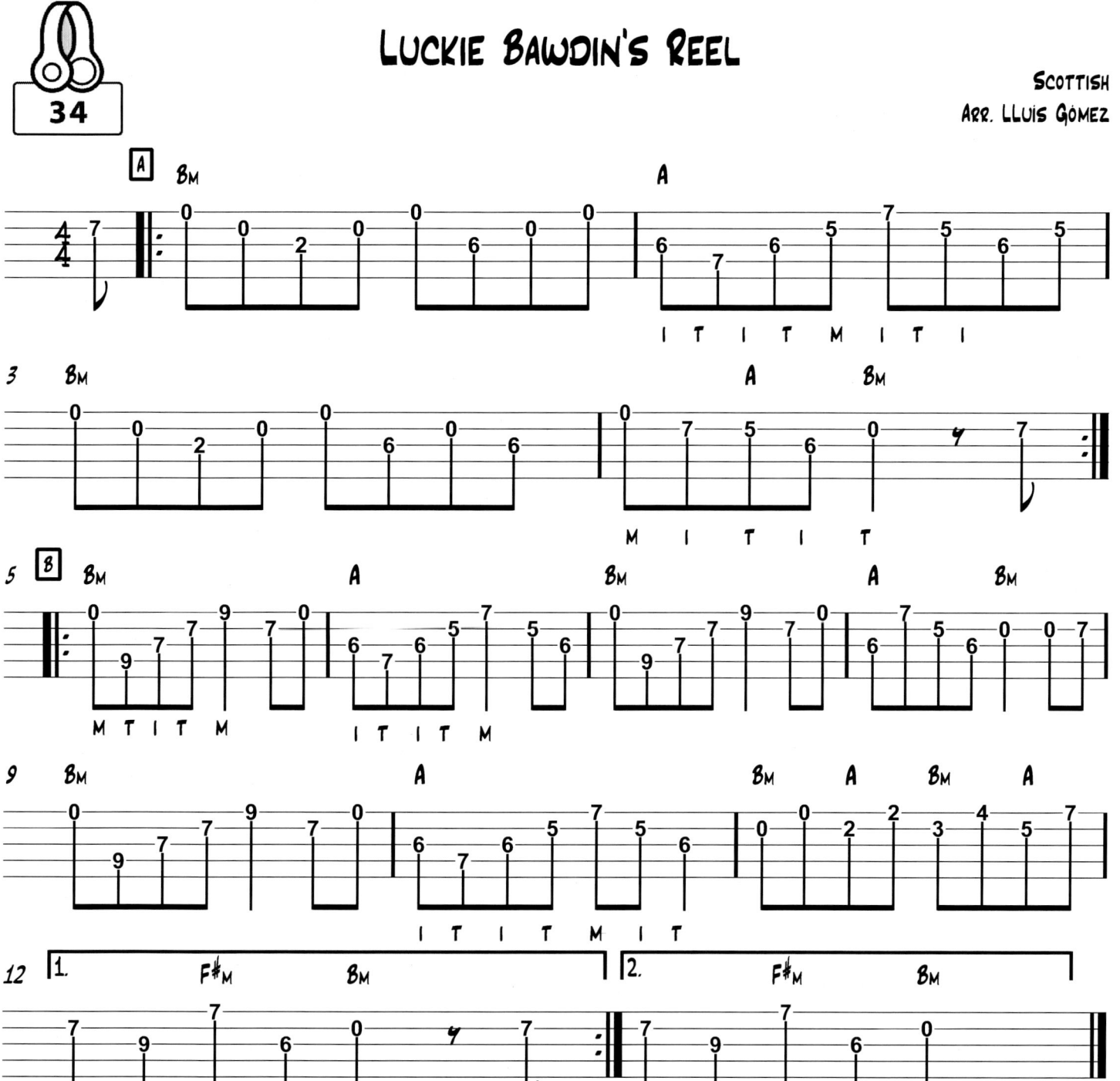

Witch of the Wave Reel

Traditional
Arr. Lluis Gómez

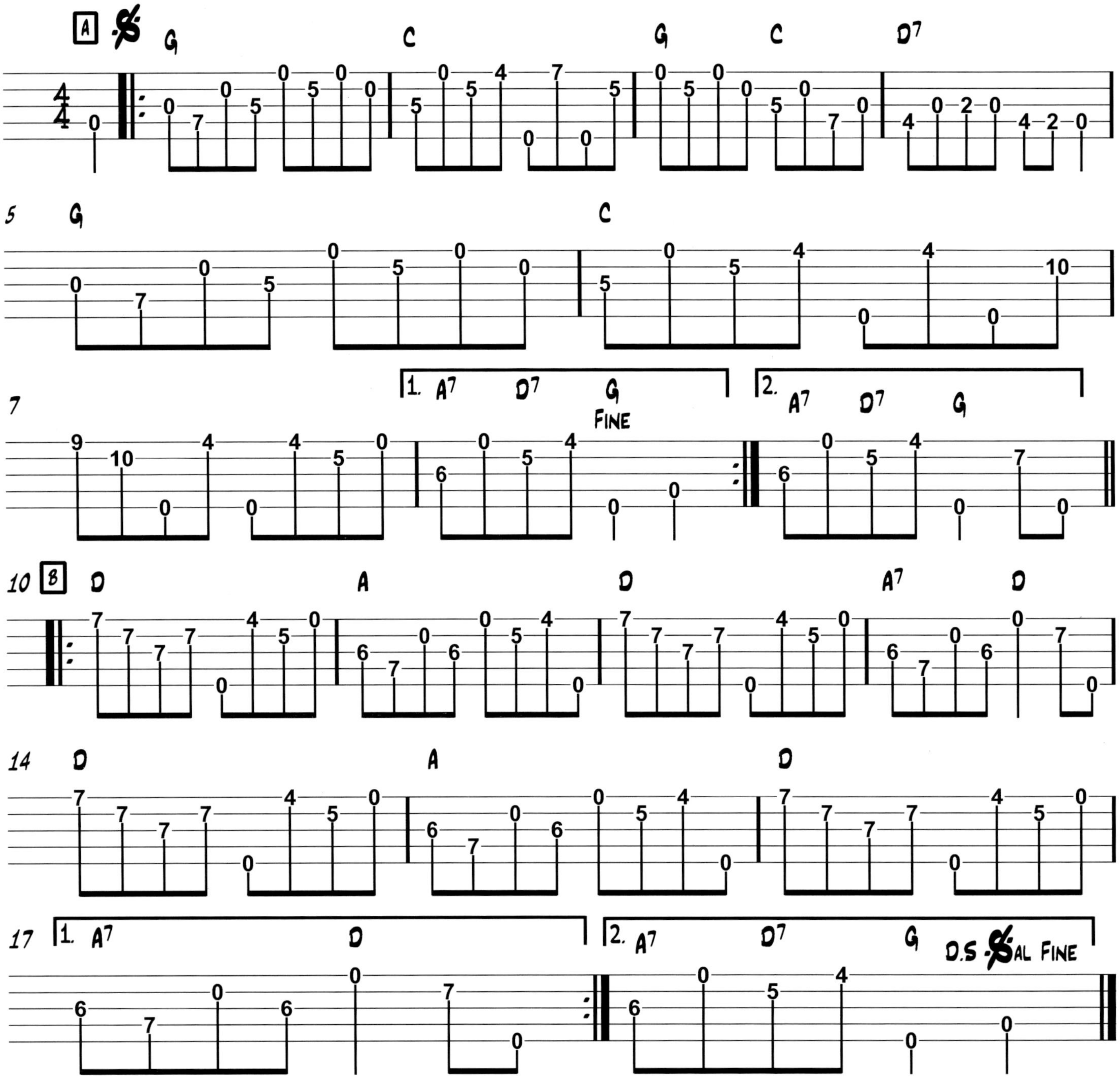

North Sea

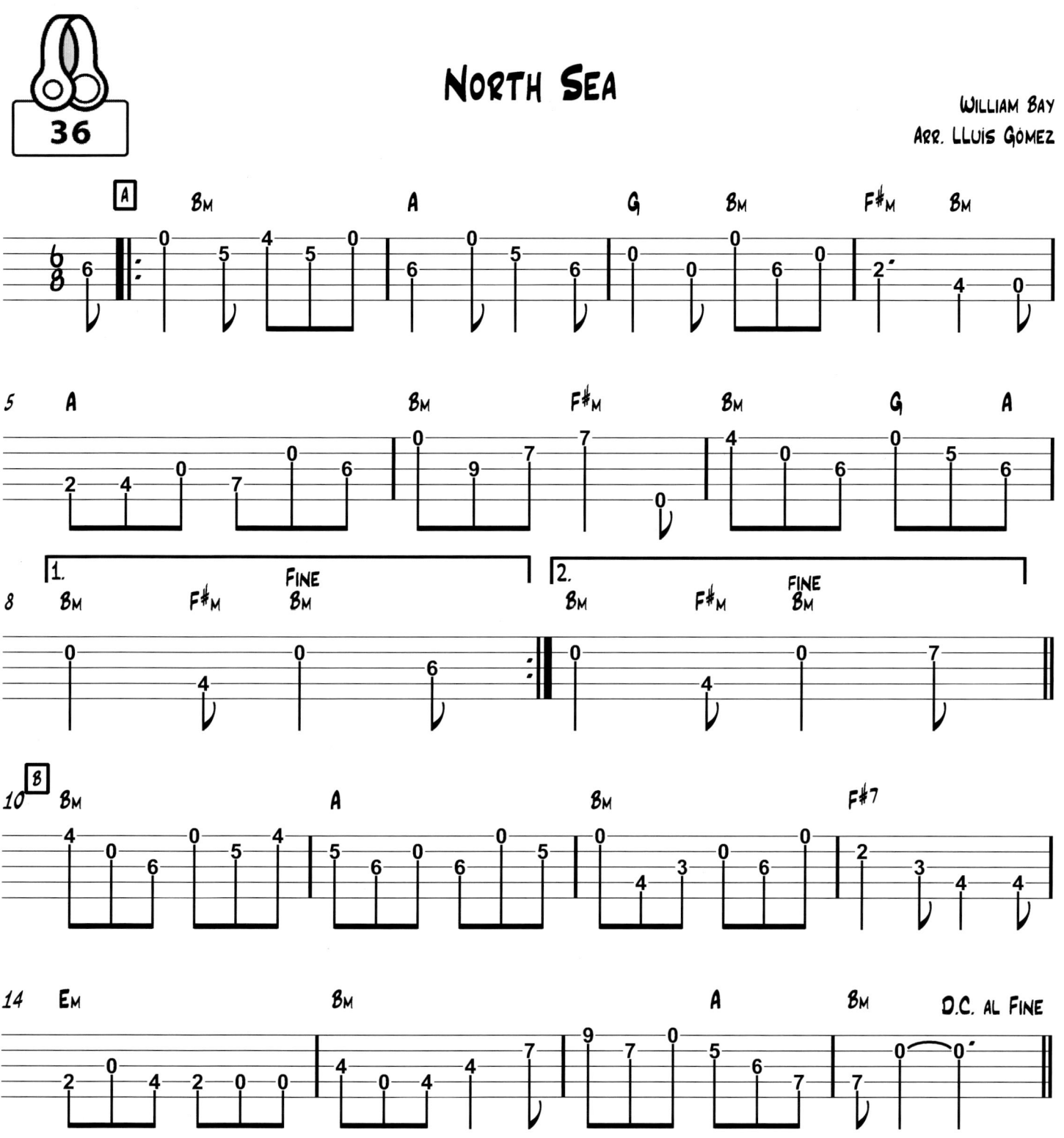

Red Haired Boy

Traditional
Arr. Lluis Gómez

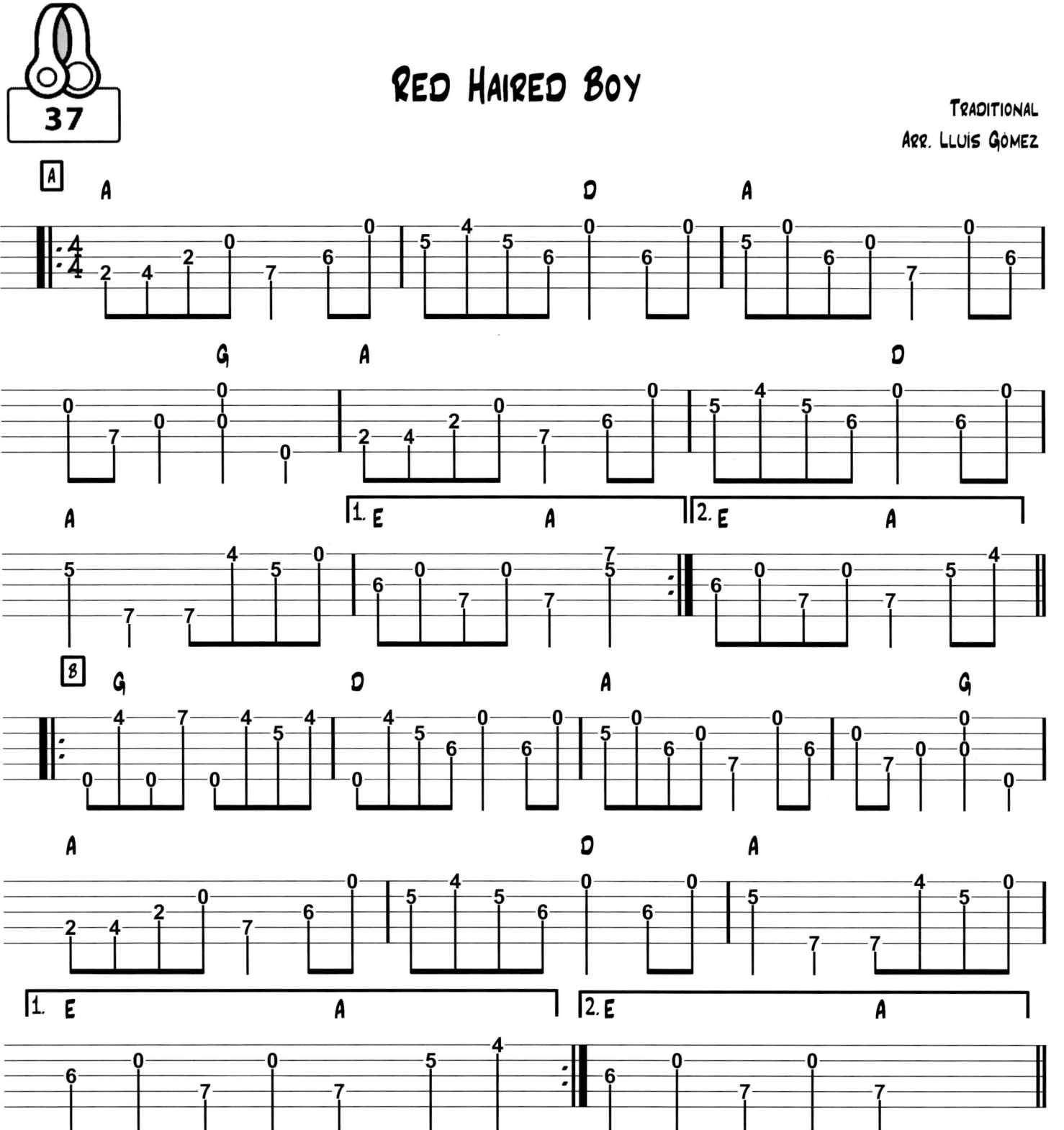

Mere Point

William Bay
Arr. Lluis Gómez

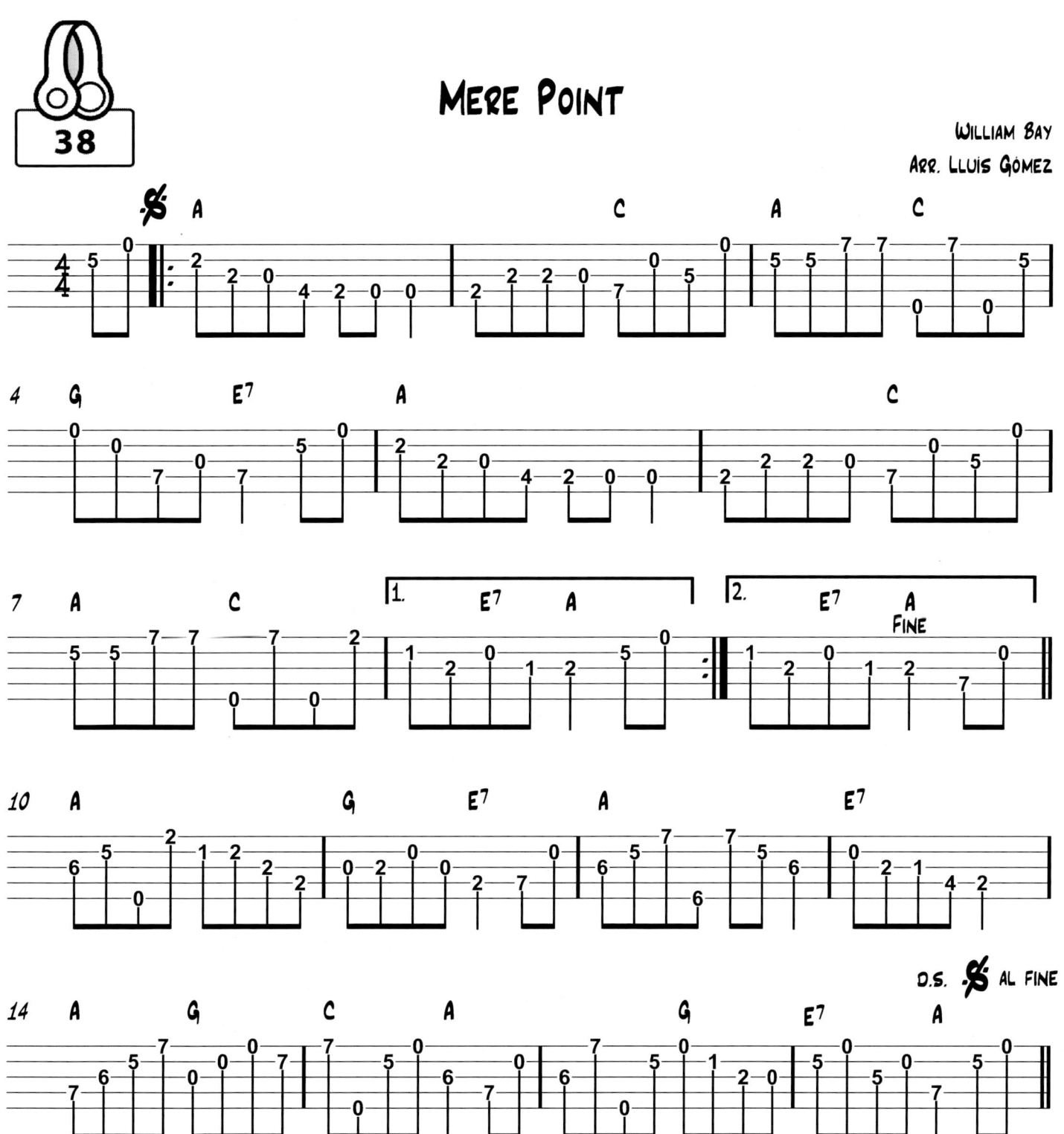

© 2020 by William Bay. All Rights Reserved.

Blackberry Blossom

Traditional
Arr. Lluís Gómez

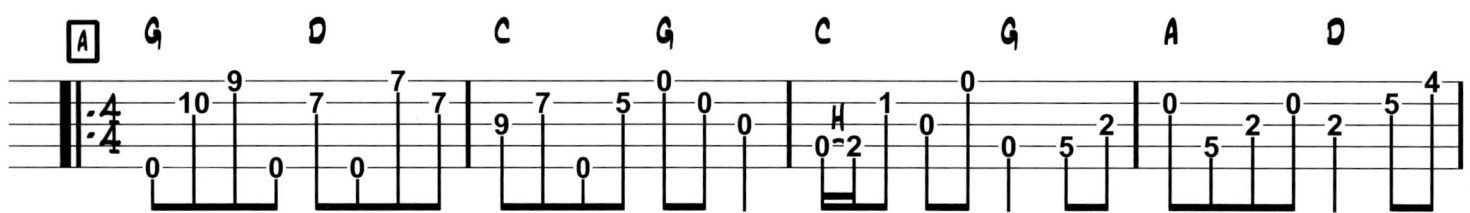
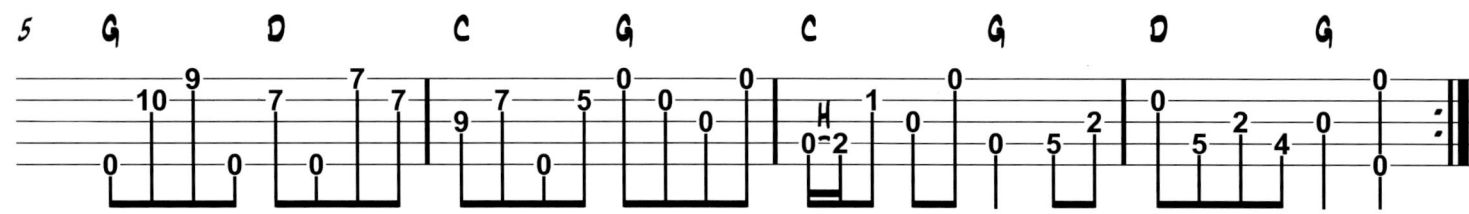
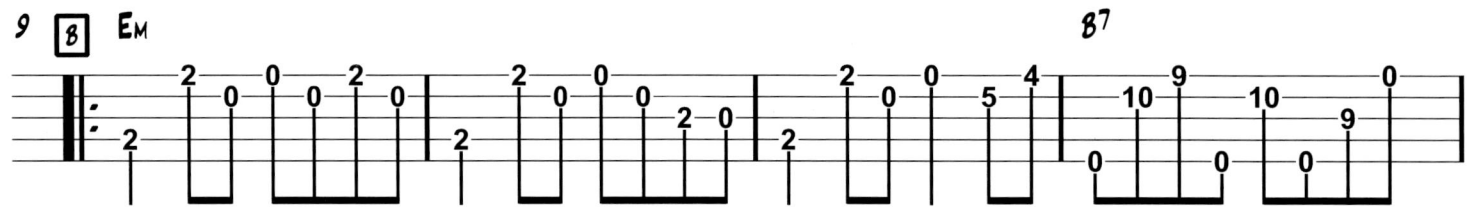
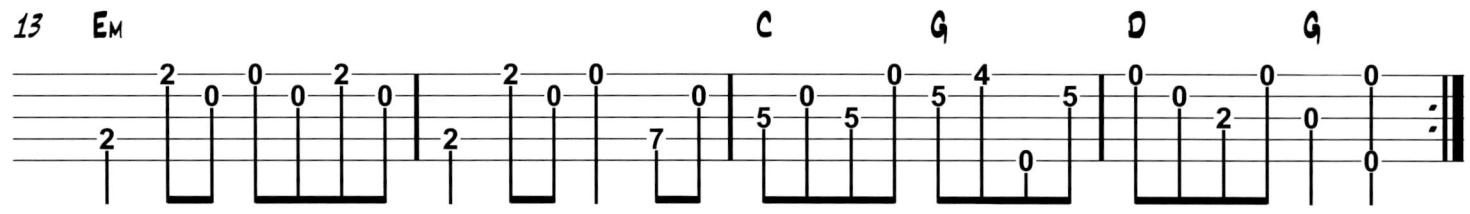

This page has been left blank to avoid an awkward page turn.

Wilson's Hornpipe

Traditional
Arr. Lluis Gómez

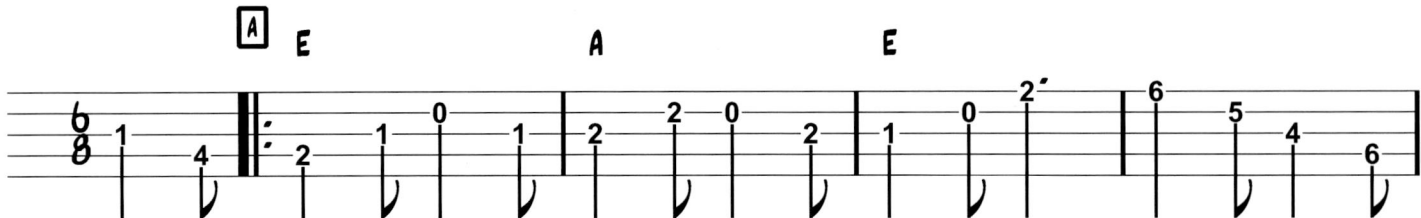
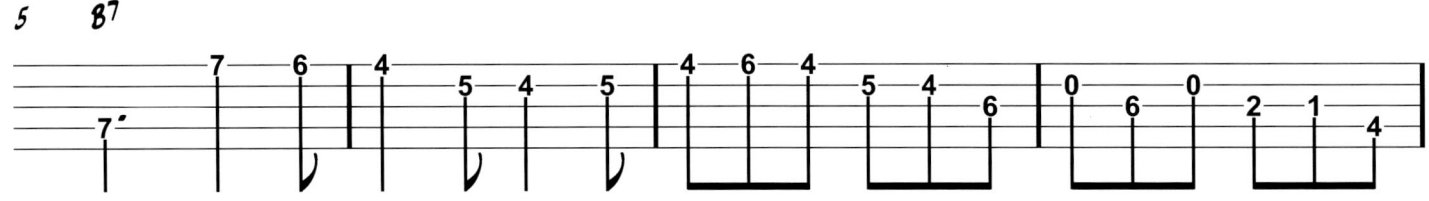
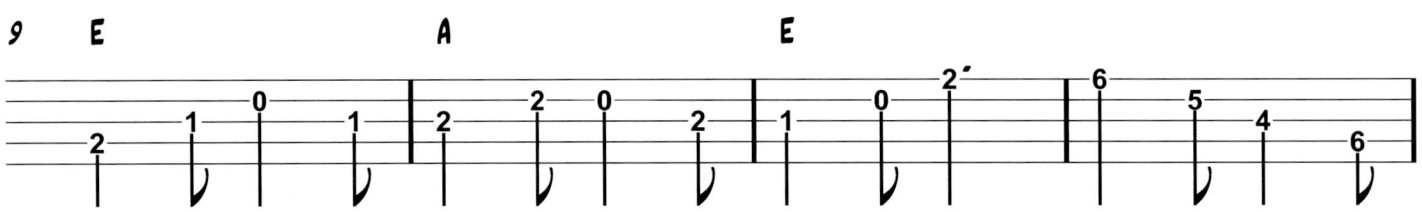
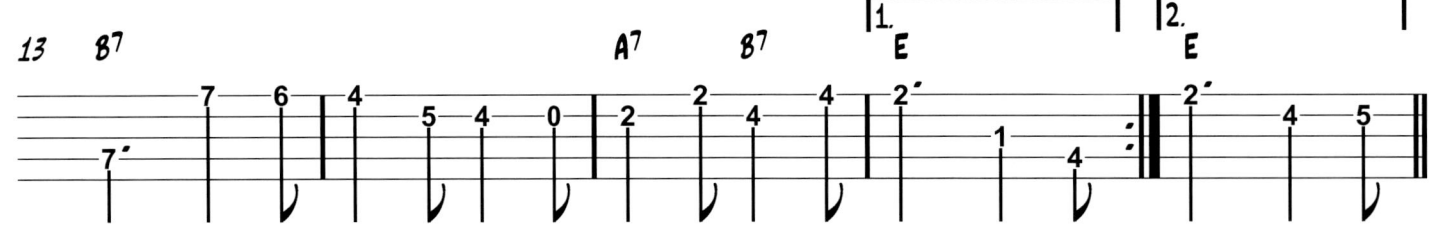

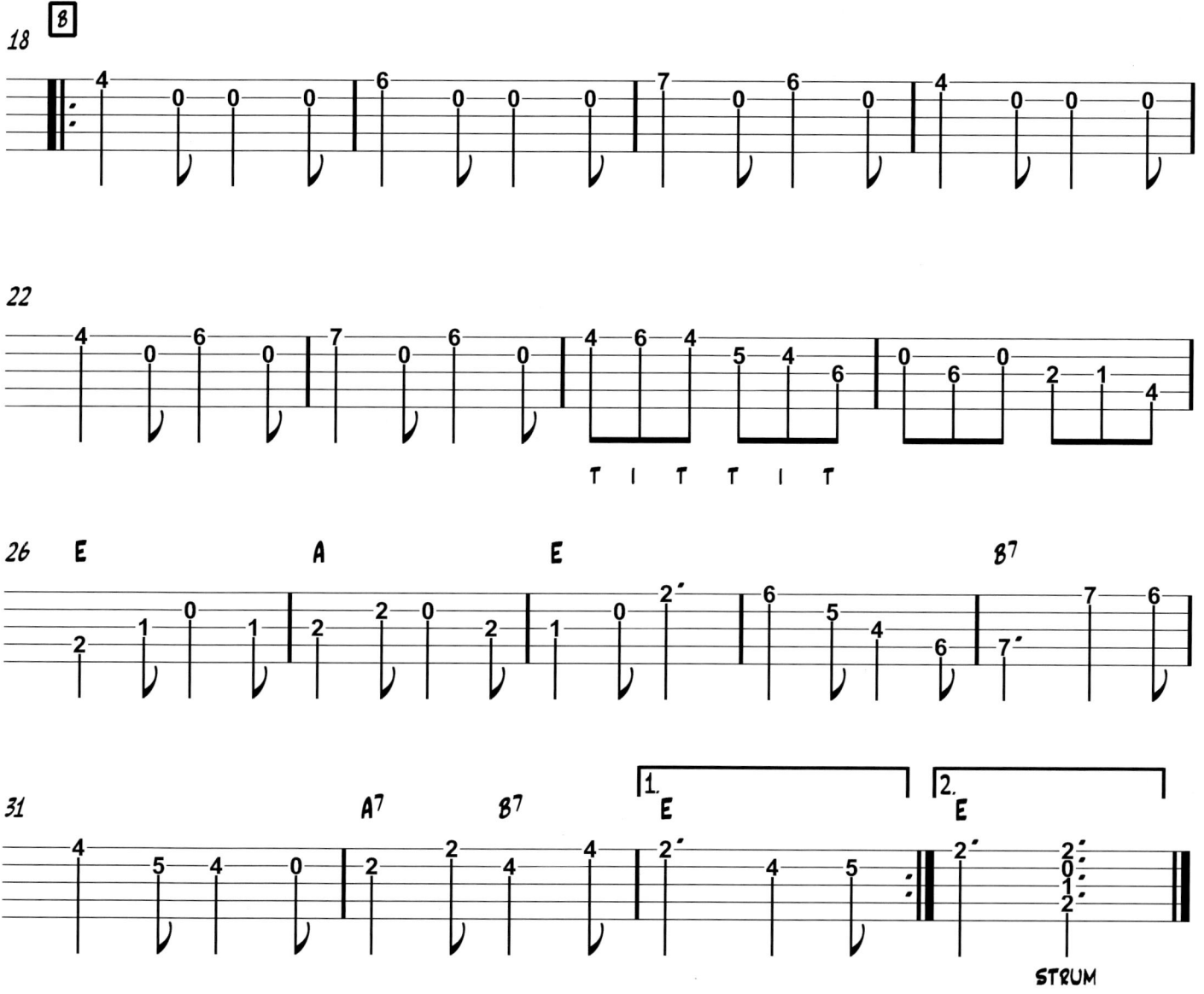

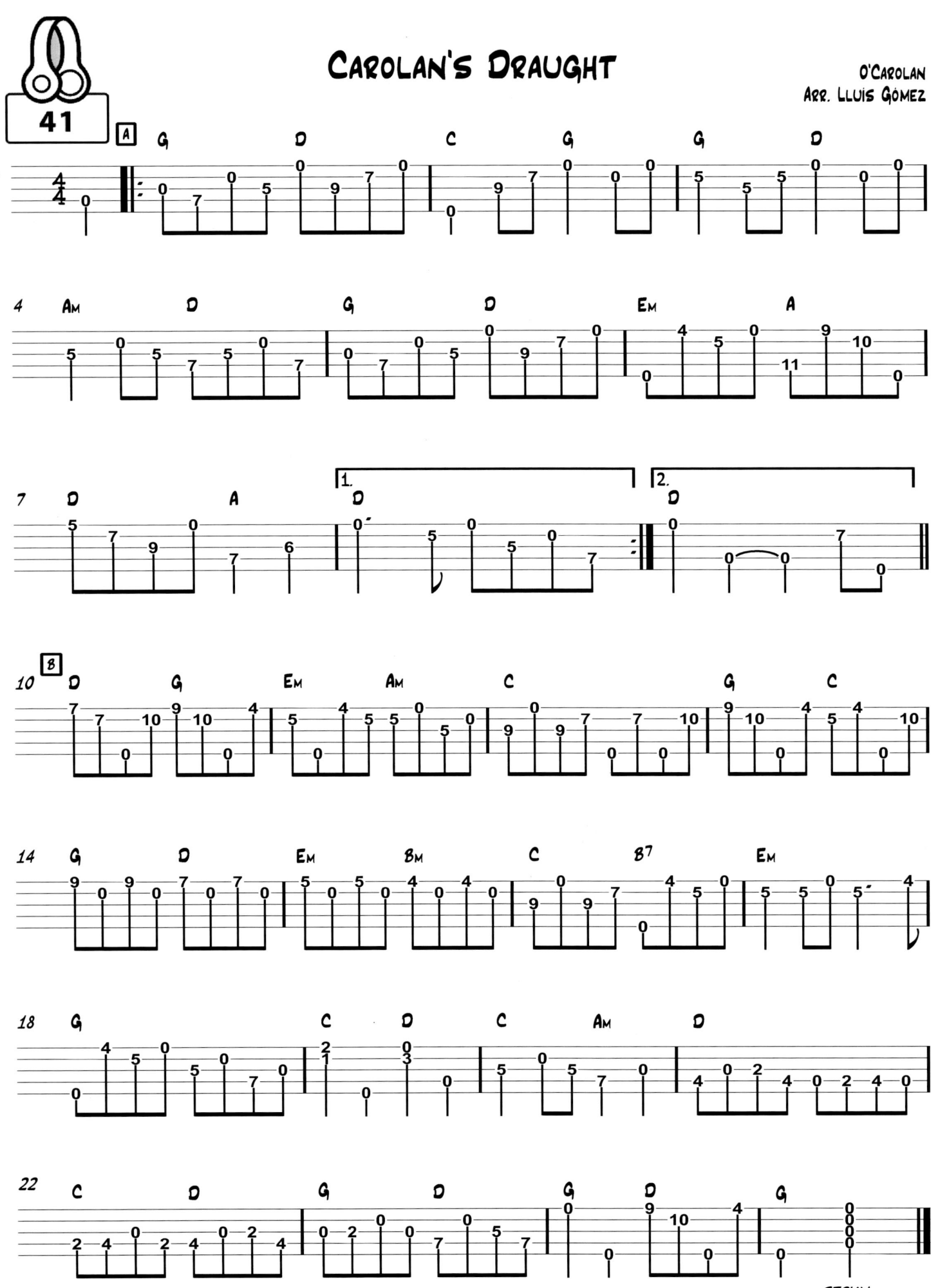

42

Days of 'Lang Syne

Scottish
Arr. Lluis Gómez

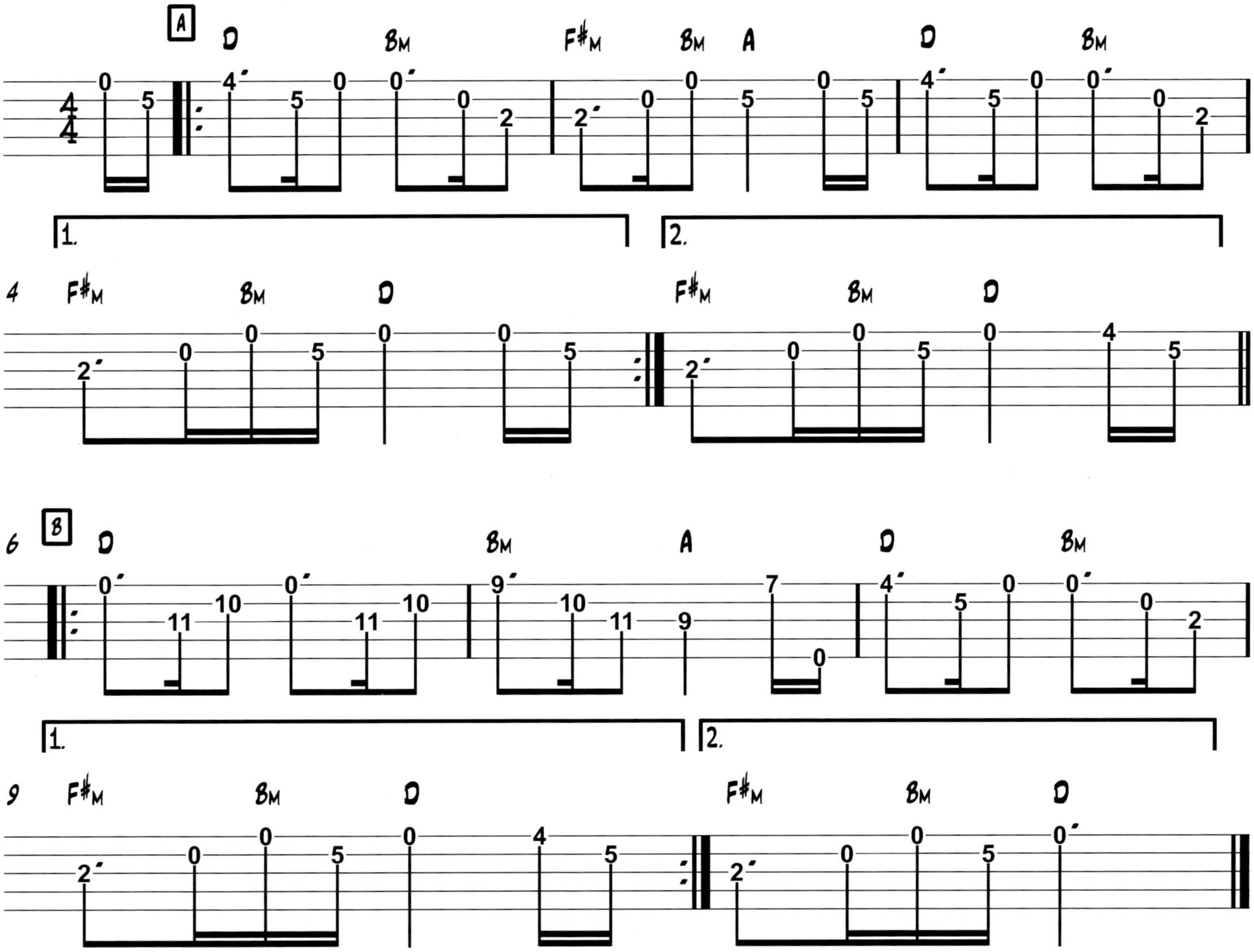

Brush Creek

William Bay
Arr. Lluis Gómez

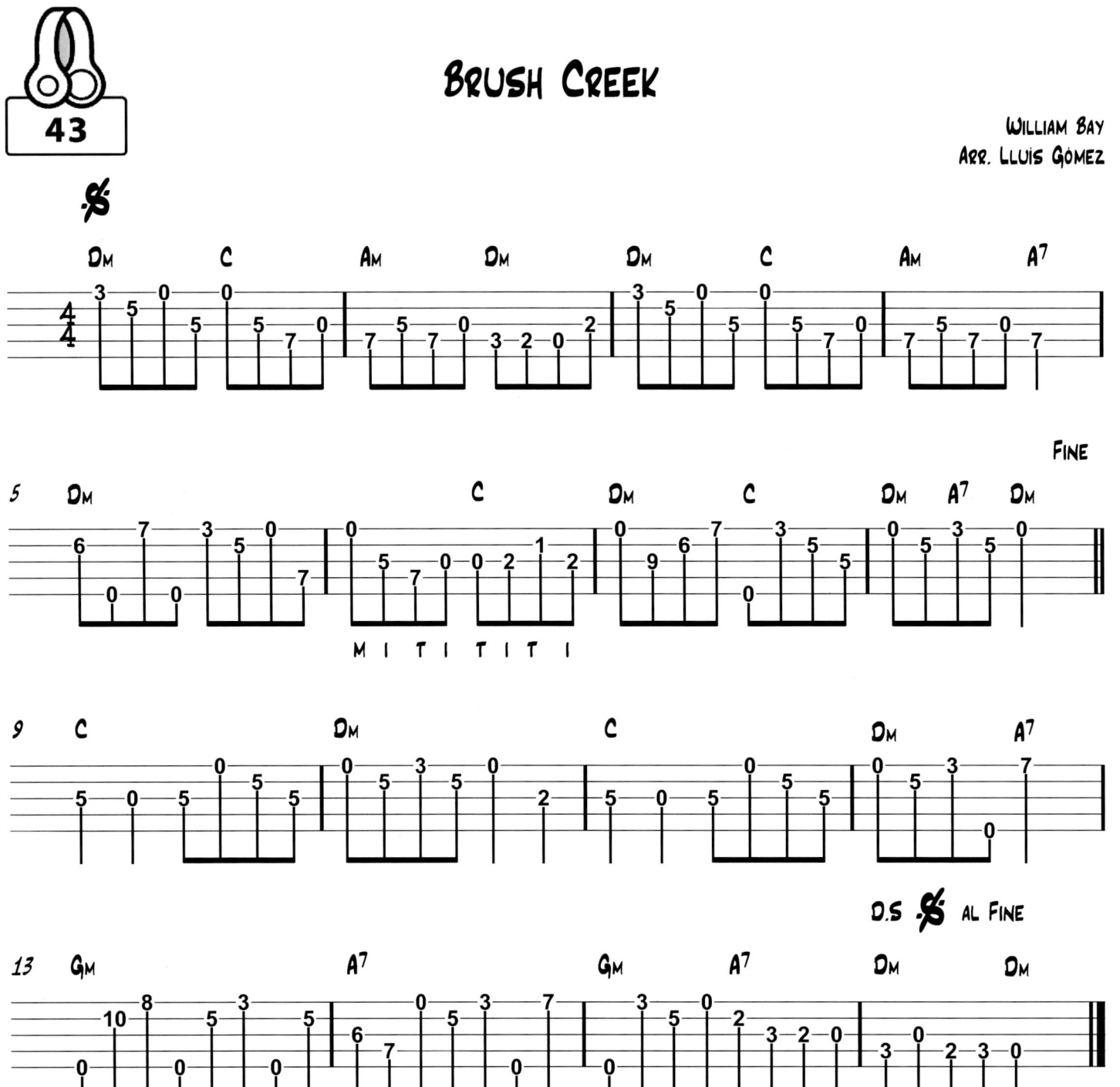

The Rights of Man

Traditional
Arr. Lluis Gómez

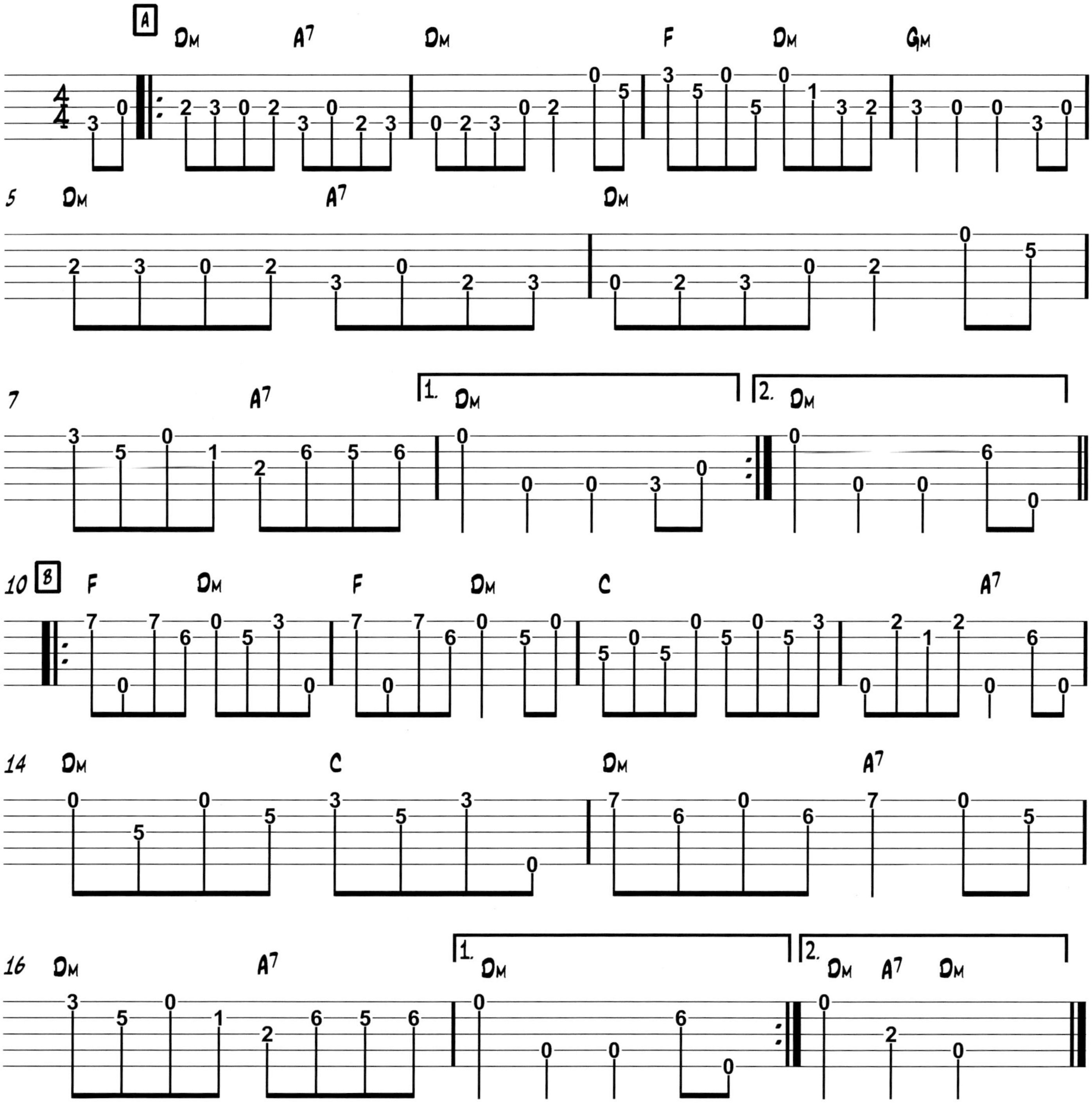

The Unfortunate Rake

Traditional
Arr. Lluis Gómez

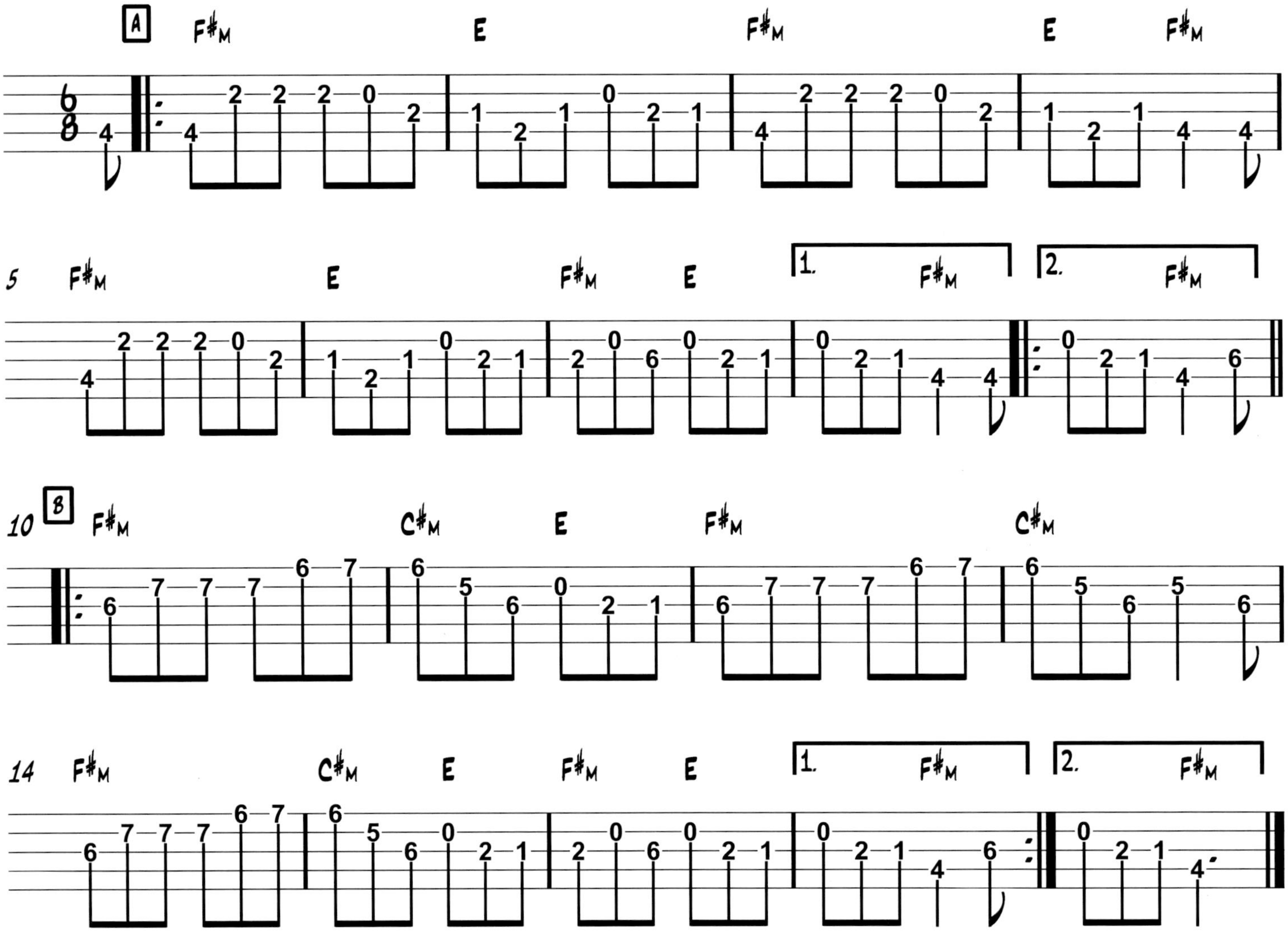

Shannon's Well

William Bay
Arr. Lluís Gómez

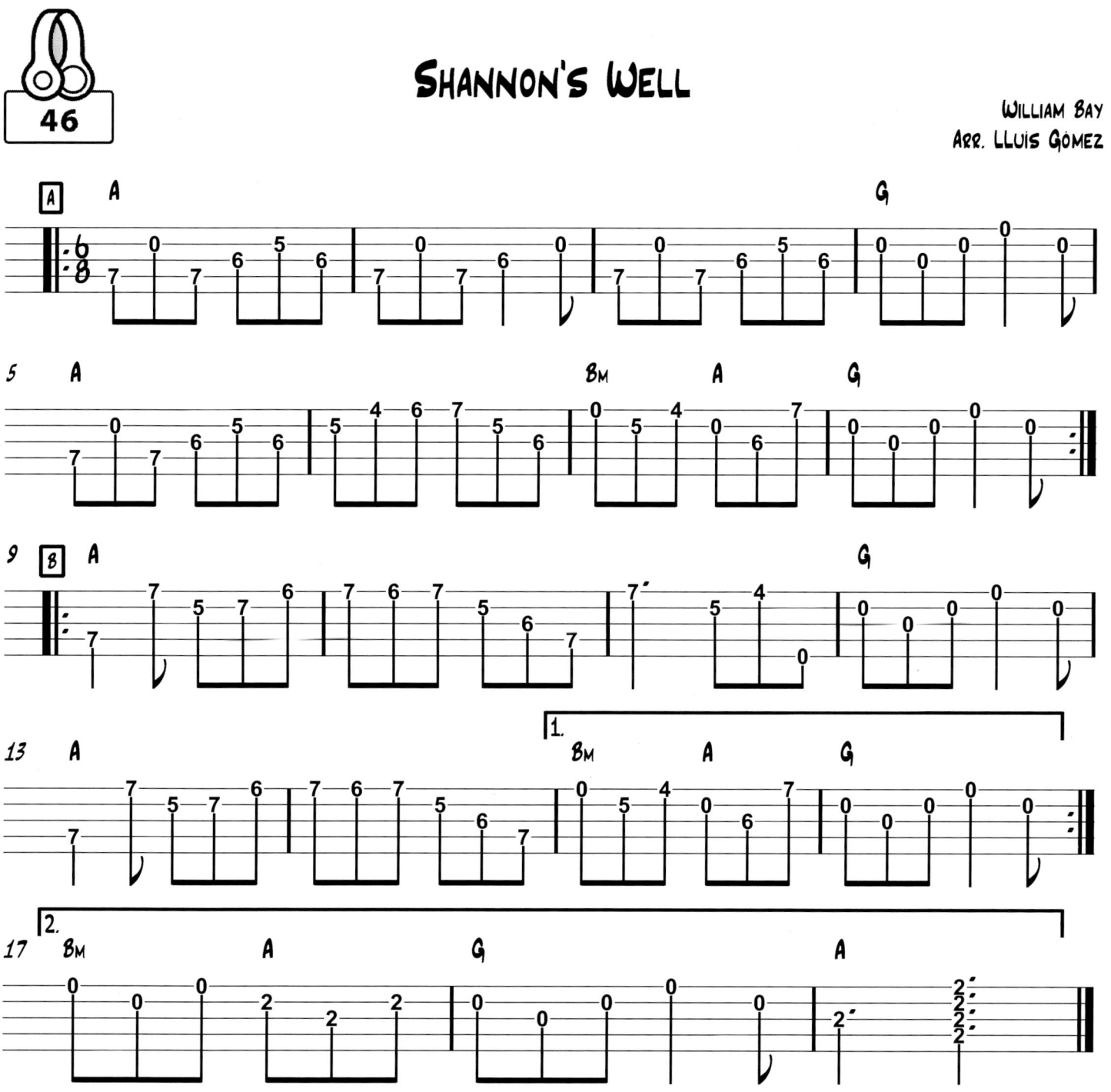

© 2020 by William Bay. All Rights Reserved.

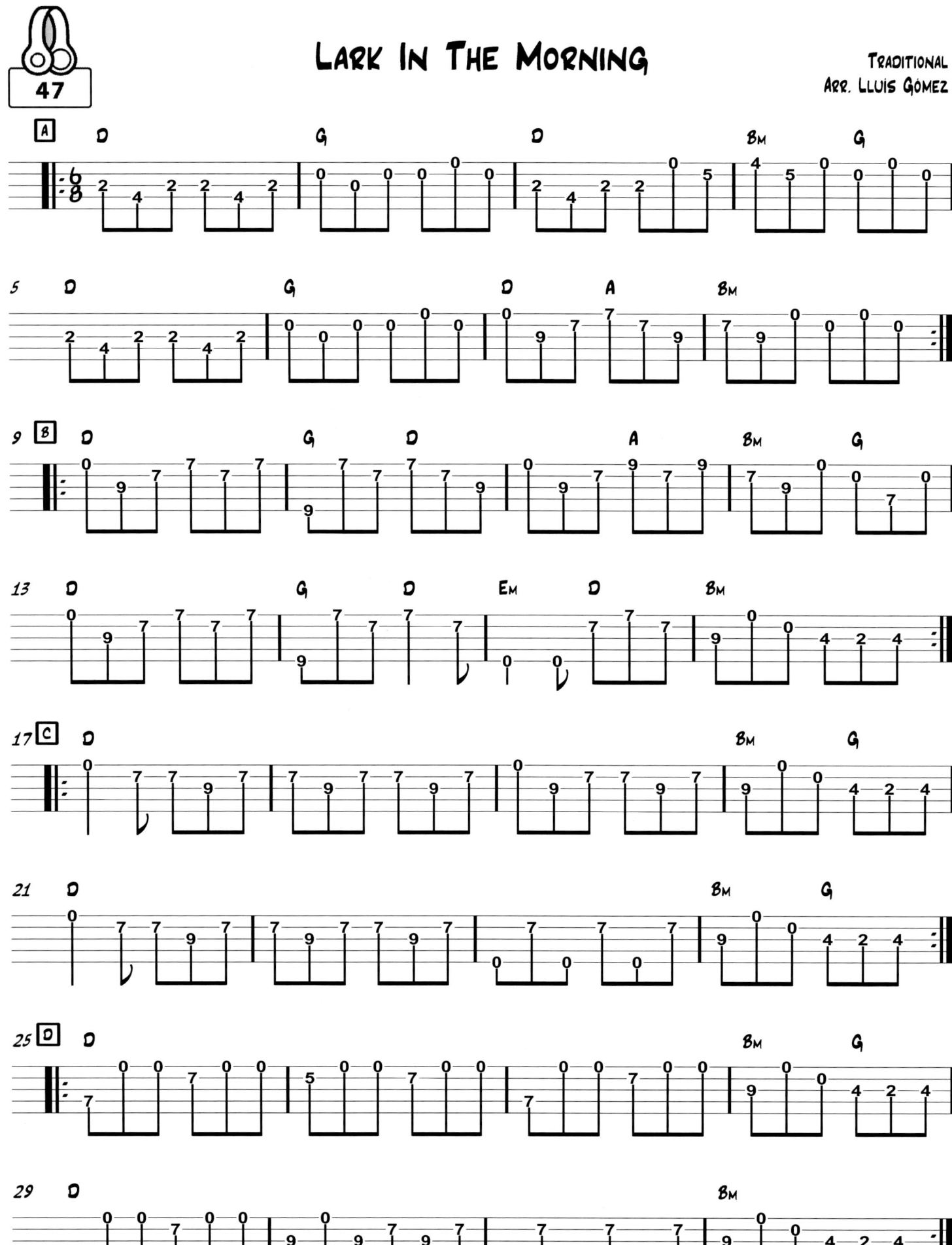

Lluís Gómez. Photo courtesy of Laura Ruiz.

At an early age and largely encouraged by the musical atmosphere in his family, Lluís Gómez taught himself to play the acoustic guitar and electric bass. He studied the flute for two years and at the age of 18, went on to study classical guitar with Pere Payes at the Music School of Premià de Mar (Spain) and electric guitar with Josep Traver. He also studied modern harmony with Ramón Montoliu at The Municipal School of Music in Badalona. At age 30 he began to teach himself fiddle, but then studied formally with Raúl Munizaga.

The discovery of bluegrass music through the *Banjo Paris Session* albums of 1975 and 1977 was a watershed in his career. He was so taken by this style that he immediately picked up the 5-string banjo and took lessons from Sedo Garcia and Ricky Araiza in Barcelona. He then travelled to France, Ireland, the United Kingdom, and the United States to take lessons from Jean Marie Redon, Bill Keith, Tony Trischka, Pete Wernick, Noam Pikelny, and Jayme Stone, among others.

In addition to recording CDs featuring his original music, Lluís has performed and recorded extensively with many artists and bands, consistently on the folk scene but also in a wide range of styles from flamenco to pop and rock music. He has also recorded the music for several films and performed in live theater productions as a musician and actor.

Widely acknowledged as a performer both in Catalunya and abroad, Lluís Gómez is one of the great connoisseurs of bluegrass music in Spain. He has written several methods for learning to play the 5-string banjo, including a bilingual Spanish-Catalan book written in collaboration with Toni Giménez. He regularly writes for several specialized magazines and in March 2015 was featured on the cover of the prestigious *Banjo NewsLetter/The 5-String Magazine*. He also plays mandolin and is the co-author with Oriol Saña of a bilingual English/Spanish book called *The Bluegrass Violin/El Violin en el Bluegrass* (Mel Bay Publications 30619M).

He directs the *Al Ras* Bluegrass & Old-Time Music Festival as well as the Barcelona Bluegrass Camp, and also teaches at the prestigious "International Stage Musique Acoustique Campus" in Virton, Belgium.

In addition to teaching at various schools, Lluís currently plays in several bluegrass, folk, and jazz manouche bands, hosts a bluegrass session in Barcelona, and regularly contributes to different media.

Index of Solos

An Comhra Donn	25
Barney's Goat	9
Bennett's Favorite Reel	31
Blackberry Blossom	40
Brighton Beach	27
Brush Creek	46
Buttermilk Jig	24
Caleb's Gorge	4
Carolan's Draught	44
Cumberland Ridge	4
Days of 'Lang Syne	45
Eighth of January	22
Eleven Mile Canyon	14
Far from Home	5
Gladiator Reel	34
Green Fields of America	28
Harvest Moon Strathspey	23
Ivy Leaf Reel	32
Jackson's Jig	17
Lark in the Morning	50
Little House 'Round the Corner	18
Luckie Bawdin's Reel	35
Mere Point	39
Missouri Mud	19
Morrison's Jig	8
National Lancer's Hornpipe	26
Neapolitan Threshers	21
North Sea	37
Red Fox Waltz	11
Red Haired Boy	38
Reel de Lapin	13
Shannon's Well	49
St. Anne's Reel	33
St. Clair's Hornpipe	29
Star of Bethlehem	30
Swallowtail Jig	7
The Burning of the Piper's Hut	15
The Clergy's Lamentation	10
The Cuckoo	9
The Downfall of Paris	12
The Rights of Man	47
The Teetotaller's Reel	6
The Unfortunate Rake	48
Whiskey Before Breakfast	20
Wilson's Hornpipe	42
Witch of the Wave Reel	36
Young McGoldrick	16